Books about Africa
by Basil Davidson

History

Current Affairs

Fiction

Can Africa Survive?

Can Africa Survive?

Arguments Against Growth Without Development

BASIL DAVIDSON

AN ATLANTIC MONTHLY PRESS BOOK

Little, Brown and Company — Boston – Toronto

FIRST EDITION

T 08/74

Library of Congress Cataloging in Publication Data

Davidson, Basil, 1914-
  Can Africa survive?

  "An Atlantic Monthly Press book."
  Includes bibliographical references.
  1. Africa, Sub-Saharan--Economic conditions.
2. Africa, Sub-Saharan--Politics and government.
3. Africa, Sub-Saharan--Social conditions. I. Title.
HC502.D3   309.1'67   74-6490
ISBN 0-316-17434-3

ATLANTIC—LITTLE, BROWN BOOKS
ARE PUBLISHED BY
LITTLE, BROWN AND COMPANY
IN ASSOCIATION WITH
THE ATLANTIC MONTHLY PRESS

Published simultaneously in Canada
by Little, Brown & Company (Canada) Limited

PRINTED IN THE UNITED STATES OF AMERICA

*To Africa's future
— and our own*

Contents

Preface

This book is offered for discussion, and is therefore deliberately, naturally, and (I hope) acutely contentious. Its reason for being so arises partly from a belief that constructive contention is the high road to clarity of thought, and partly from a similarly deep conviction that the problems of Africa now call more demandingly than at any previous time, even than during the time of the Atlantic slave trade, even than during the time of colonial invasion and subjection, for the questioning of familiar attitudes and orthodoxies. And by the problems of Africa I mean to refer, of course, as much to the nature of Africa's relations with "our" world, and so, at least by direct implication, to the nature and condition of "our" societies that are called "developed," as to any of the situations inherent to Africa itself. Today we are all in the same boat in a sense that was never true before, even though some are still traveling in the first class and many in the steerage.

So much for form: as to content, this inquiry derives from a historical approach to modern Africa, primarily Africa south of the Sahara, and draws a number of general conclusions from examples which seem particularly revealing. No such book could be comprehensive in its coverage, and would be quite unreadable if it tried to be; yet I believe that my examples do not misrepresent the general evidence, although that too could be a matter for discussion. If the title appears unduly rhetorical, my answer is that the present condition of affairs, whether "there" or "here," whether "underdeveloped" or "developed," can justify the loudest cry of titular button-holing.

These pages take their rise from lectures delivered during 1972 at the University of Edinburgh, where I had the honor to be Montague Burton Visiting Professor of International Relations; and I wish to thank the Court of the University of Edinburgh for their permission to publish, as well as members of the History Department and of the African Studies Centre for their similar encouragement and friendship. This in no way implies that anyone save myself is responsible for what follows here.

Can Africa Survive?

CHAPTER ONE

A Continental Crisis

That the great difference between "rich countries" and "poor countries" lies in the first having solved their basic problems, and in the second having failed, is a view of the world no longer argued with much conviction, at least in serious debate. In what "rich country," after all, do you now find any large agreement that basic problems have been solved, even are being solved? All the same, this is still a view of the world that governs current orthodoxy of policy and action, especially in wide segments of the "development industry." There you are still likely to be told that "their development" need only follow the same course as "ours," and all will then be well. "We" know best, and so let "them" follow.[1]

In their crudest forms, no doubt, such attitudes are an overhang of colonial paternalism. They go hand-in-hand with others equally familiar, such as the identification of civilized progress with technological complexity, as though the truest measure of a society's improvement were to be found in the growth of its traffic jams. More subtly, these attitudes betray an oddly provincial belief that "the way we live in the West" is the way that everyone else ought to live, and that "our system" is the only right and proper future for mankind.

These convictions may now seem greatly open to question. The fact remains that they and their underlying motivations have gone far to form the general culture of the "advanced" countries, and even, here and there, the general culture of the "backward" countries. If nothing else, they have given rise to a large number of misunderstandings about the nature of the problems of Africa, as of the problems of any other part of the "Third World." These problems are thus presented, and widely accepted, as arising chiefly from a failure to develop what already exists: from a failure, that is, to enlarge and expand an existing social and economic structure which, being enlarged and expanded, will duly become a viable and reliable means of general progress. And this failure, in turn, is then attributed to the weakness of this or that regime, the corruption of this or that individual, the dissidence of this or that group, or simply the fecklessness of populations "who do not live as we live."

All this seems to be a total misconception of how things really are. The problems of politically independent Africa (or of still-colonial Africa) arise in no essential way from a failure to develop what already exists. This is because what already exists, in the sense of socio-economic system or articulated national structure, is not capable of development, cannot become a viable means of general progress, offers no reliable foundation for a better future.

What already exists, in this meaning and context, is

4

either an inheritance from a world that is past, or the merely peripheral fragment or fragments of an international system built and controlled for the benefit of non-Africans. On the one hand, the past cannot be recalled, however valid it may once have been. On the other, these peripheral fragments cannot be made to develop: cannot of themselves, that is, lead to systems which will be viable and expansive because they will also be self-generating, sovereign in their choice of options, and independent in their capacity to change.

Of course these fragments can be made to grow in size. They can become more productive. A thousand plans and projects tell us so, and with serried ranks of statistics. Yet it happens to be one of the harder lessons of modern times, hammered home repeatedly during the 1960s, that growth is by no means necessarily the same as development, and may indeed be quite the reverse of development. Thus the annual quantity of cocoa produced in Ghana during the past ten years or so has repeatedly passed all previous records. But so has Ghana's annual burden of foreign indebtedness, and, in consequence, Ghana's helplessness within the general system that was shaped in colonial times.

Still less are the real problems of independent Africa a matter of "little local difficulties": of the frictions which attend upon the exercise of political self-rule after a long period of direct foreign domination, of the momentary upsurge of this or that discontent and factional demand, or of the irresponsibility of this or that leader and leading group. They may be all these things; in any case they are also much more than these things, and different from them.

Africa's real problems are those of a period of major transition from systems of development viable in the precolonial past to other systems, similarly viable, which can face the challenges of the future. No transition on such a scale can be short or easy; in Africa's case the difficulties are increased, even vastly increased, by the contrary interests of the international system which still encloses the continent, if with a degree of overall control that varies in time and place.

The crisis which thus arises is, therefore, one of institutions. Those of the past have lost their containing power. Those of the present offer little save confusion. Those of the future have yet to appear. And it is this that gives all these societies, all these collections of communities, their essential unity of situation, no matter how different they otherwise may be among themselves or within themselves. In this respect, like it or not, they share the same plight. Each of them has to cross the same tempestuous flood between what now appears as the firm land of the remote past and the assurance of firm land in the future.

Thus united, they are also joined in the contradictions of their situation. That is what makes the drama that may now be seen on every hand. Wherever you may look today, from one end of the continent to the other, you will find upheaval or new initiative alongside the still persisting stagnation of many decades: hope in company with the absence of hope; determination striving with indifference; stubborn effort to get things moving forward even when the direction proves wrong, the captain incapable, the crew dispersed; and also, more than may easily appear, the striving for creative change even when the means of achieving it are perilously small or fragile.

The examples are legion, even though little noticed in the outside world, or, when noticed, little understood.

In the central plains of Tanzania, in a region of persistent drought and small fertility about the size of half of Scotland, there live a people called the waGogo who have repeatedly suffered famine at the worst of seasons and considerable discomfort at the best. They have lived there for a long time, certainly for several centuries, and have scarcely ever had enough water for comfort and security.

Yet the evidence, such as we have it, suggests that the water shortage has become worse for the waGogo over recent decades, if only because the numbers of this people have grown steadily larger, while the way of life of the waGogo, for want of any suitable alternative, has remained almost exactly as it was before. They have continued to live within the patterns of their ancient settlement and tradition, inhabiting small and isolated homestead groups spread far and wide across their plains.

Living like this, they have found it difficult, or impossible, to combine together in any way which would enable them to share in such meager modernizing facilities as have become available, whether in the form of schools, clinics, or mechanically improved water facilities. The colonial authorities of the Trusteeship era — the period from 1919 to 1961 — found it unnecessary to do much or anything about the problems of the waGogo, while the independent government that emerged in December 1961 found it impossible. But in 1971 the waGogo decided to begin living in a different way. They had been lately offered an alternative that might help them, and they were ready to give it a try.

The government and its national party, the Tanzanian African National Union, had urged upon them the advantages that might accrue from ceasing to live in scattered homesteads or little hamlets lost in the bush, and from starting to live in more or less large villages — *ujamaa* villages, self-help villages which, they were promised, the government would help them to build and furnish with water wells and other community facilities.

All this ran counter to their cherished customs and beliefs. If the waGogo had continued to live in the manner of their ancestors, this was because, in distant days, the manner of their ancestors had proved its worth. Having proved its worth, it had given rise to a culture which found virtue in physical isolation and small-group self-sufficiency. What was now said to them was not that a new and different way of living — emphasizing community and cooperation — was or would be in some inherent sense better than the old. What was said was that the old way had become untenable.

In 1971 a few waGogo heeded this advice, driven as they were by the memory and prospect of famine. These few, it seems, found substance in the government's promises. However justifiably skeptical of an authority so far remote from their own, they were not entirely disappointed. And word went back to the isolated homesteads and hamlets, out there beyond the skyline of the inland hills, that there might indeed be an alternative to trekking weary miles for pots of water, or to watching handfuls of thin cattle lose what little weight they had as bushland simmered in the rainless heat. And in May of that year, displaying a characteristically African capacity for adjusting to circumstances entirely new or unforeseen, and denying their ingrained conservatism, the waGogo made up their mind to move as a whole people. By mid-July no fewer than 200,000 of them, practically their ethnic total, appear to have taken this decision.

They waited for the ripening of their crops, and, then, as soon as they had gathered in their meager harvest, they "tore down their houses, salvaging whatever might be useful, gathered their few scanty possessions, and sat and waited for trucks to move them."[2]

The government, on this occasion not unreasonably, was taken by surprise. It had called these people to a new and cooperative pattern of life, just as it had called every other of the country's many ethnic groups. But nothing had suggested any likely response on this scale. On the contrary, everything had indicated that countryside conservatism would long ignore the alternative thus glowingly set forth.

And then, suddenly, there they were — a multitude of peasants sitting by the roadside, waiting for transport to new villages and wells and huts and farming land. The mere survival of the government's whole policy, let alone its eventual success, turned on meeting these expectations. Reacting to this emergency, the government mobilized whatever it could. "Every water-drilling rig in the country was diverted to the region, almost every water bowser was called in, and tractors were pulled off State farms to clear the [necessary] land"; while President Julius Nyerere himself, well seeing the nature of the test, moved up from the capital into one of the co-

9

operative villages of the region, built the year before, and stayed there for a month — making bricks as an exercise in intelligent publicity, but, much more, supervizing the work of moving families into new quarters. By the end of August it appeared that about half this people could be and even would be resettled in new communities, during 1971, with secure shelter and water, while the others might follow in the rest of 1971 and in 1972. By August, the total of new villages was climbing towards 200. In the circumstances it was probably enough, if narrowly enough, to prove to this people that the government had meant what it said, and to provide a sufficiently useful demonstration of the advantages that could be made to accrue from community and cooperation. And the waGogo, it seems, thought so too, for they continued to move into new villages. Within the larger crisis they were trying to adjust to their own. The story of this attempt was not to be without its traumas and disappointments, and others in Tanzania have since proved more fruitful. Their example is, in any case, characteristic of many such attempts today.

At about the same time as the waGogo were sitting by the dirt roads of the Dodoma plains, or grappling with the problems of settling into village life, another and in some ways still more dramatic effort at constructive change could be observed in progress about a thousand miles to the westward. Here in eastern Angola, other rural peoples even further removed from what we may call the modern world, even closer to the beliefs and behavior of a distant African past, were also beginning to live in a new way, or, at least, according to new ideas and organizational patterns. These peoples —

Mbunda, Luchazi, Luvale, Lunda, Chokwe, and others —
were now attempting to change their circumstances and
their prospects by uniting together in a multi-ethnic network of representative committees of a new kind, not
known among them before; by accepting a common
leadership within a new concept of community and cooperation; by confronting Portuguese colonial armies
with an army of their own; and, generally, by adhering
to a range of objectives and disciplines designed to
achieve a far-reaching change in the way they live.

Superficially, of course, the crisis in Angola — as in
Portuguese-colonized Mozambique and Guiné, where
the same process could and can be observed — was and
is crudely colonial. These peoples have organized themselves under a leadership vowed to remove Portuguese
rule and the structures imposed by it. But they have also
organized themselves, or are in course of doing so, in
ways that suppose a large historical development of the
structures and assumptions of their own history: a development, that is, which supposes systemic change; and
this, of course, is where their true importance will in the
long run be found to lie.

Moving among them, one can see this attempt to build
the new from the old in a multitude of different ways,
and in everyday experience. The authority of elders, buttressed by ancestral sanction, is still there. All the same,
it gradually gives way to the authority of elective committees which, though sometimes still manned by elders
and inspired by traditional beliefs, gradually displace the
old ancestral sanctions by powers drawn from an entirely
different order of ideas. The explanations of religion, de-
pending on ancestral guidance made manifest at shrines

and in priestly consultations, are also still there; and, to some extent at least, will long remain there. Yet they too, however venerable and prestigious, are also gradually displaced by explanations drawn from quite different kinds of knowledge. Thus the bullets of the Portuguese cannot be defeated by charms and spells, but, as people have learned, only in quite different ways; and one enlightenment, however particular it may be, leads on to others; and others, accumulating a new wisdom, begin to body forth a new society.

So it is that people there begin to talk a new political language, to think about their communities in new ways, to embark on forms of cooperation not practiced before. They, too, are dealing with a crisis which marks a historical turning point, no matter what the precise outcome may prove to be. They, too, are a part and even perhaps a central part of the ongoing pattern of change, of attempted change, which Africa now demonstrates, if often beneath the public or reported surface of events, or against the tide of established policy and guidance.

Such examples may be thought extreme. Yet their qualities of being extreme do not really make them uncharacteristic in the wider scene. One could think of many other examples whose difference from these would at first sight be very great, but whose underlying meaning and effect are of much the same order. In the new component states of northern Nigeria which have taken shape since 1967, the displacement of emirate authority, of traditional authority, by new elective councils may not look like revolution: all the same, it is certainly more than mere reform. The old native authorities are not being reformed; they are being done away with and displaced by elective authorities. All this is part of a general process that may be gradual rather than abrupt, may meet with setbacks, may be long in the completion. This process is nonetheless a grappling with problems of transition between radically different forms and concepts. And to that extent it is exemplary of Africa's central problem, of this continental crisis of system and structure that now confronts all these peoples in one degree of intensity or another.

And then, again, underlining the fact and general nature of this crisis, there is what may be called the negative evidence: the evidence which is provided by the very instability of existing regimes and governments, and which goes to confirm the failure of existing institutions to meet the needs they are supposed to serve and fulfill.

Since 1957, the year of Ghana's independence, first of its kind south of Sudan, a multitude of more or less violent and in any case unconstitutional changes of government, or attempts at such, have shaken the institutions set in place at the time of colonial withdrawal. And of these upheavals, about a score have abolished civilian or constitutional rule in favor of more or less overt forms of autocracy or oligarchy, even if these are sometimes masked by a show of democratic ceremonial.

Could there be, one may ask, a more convincing demonstration of the inadequacy of the institutions set in place at the time of colonial withdrawal? Could any sequence of events more clearly illustrate a drastic but also general breakdown in the means of self-realization and sociocultural development? What does this military scramble for power, whether by colonels or corporals, really show — if not a landscape of political and social frustration?

Whether by the positive evidence of efforts to change what exists, or by the negative evidence of attempts to save what exists from still further collapse, the picture that now builds up is one that has coherence on a central point: it reveals an institutional failure which is profound, present everywhere, and beyond the remedial power of any mere modification or reform.

The system or the systems, as they stand, simply do not work; and, apparently, cannot be made to work. In 1966 Kwame Nkrumah was evicted from Ghana on the grounds that his radical policies had ruined the country. There followed a period of military-police rule under General Joseph Ankrah and Mr. John Harlley, and then a return to parliamentary government under Dr. Kofi Busia and his Progress party. This latter period was marked by the most careful application of policies which were the reverse of radical; and Dr. Busia and his government were loudly applauded in London and Washington. But what happened? Within two years Dr. Busia and his regime were overthrown by Colonel Ignatius Acheampoug on the grounds that his conservative policies had ruined the country. And the evidence adduced against Dr. Busia was a great deal more painful than the evidence adduced against Dr. Nkrumah. Not only was Ghana still more cripplingly in debt to foreign lenders by the end of the Busia regime, but the harshest pressures of foreign usury came not from debts incurred under Nkrumah but from debts incurred under Busia, and it was these new debts, above all, which forced a huge devaluation of the Ghana currency.[3]

When the United States dollar is devalued by 5 percent or so, or the British pound by the same amount, we are informed that the whole grand superstructure of world monetary control is in danger of chaos or disintegration. What can one think of the viability of an African monetary system in which the currency of Ghana had to be devalued, overnight, by 44 percent?

Whatever immediate reasons for such desperate measures may be adduced, this continental crisis of institutions has a historical dimension which reaches far back into the past, just as we may think that it will also reach a long way into the future.

An attentive reading of the historical evidence, it seems to me, displays a latent institutional breakdown started even before the colonial period began. Its origins, on this view, will be found in Late Iron Age structures of society and systems of production whose capacity for further expansion, or growth, was nearing its possible limit even by the early part of the nineteenth century. There is much to show, if still in a tentative and uncrystallized way, that some or even many of these systems and structures then became the victims, as it were, of their past success.

Their enlargement over previous centuries had enabled a steady growth and spread of population, on rising if still low levels of technology and command of environment, in all habitable zones of the continent, as well as in some that were habitable only by a narrow margin of survival. Over perhaps a thousand years before the nineteenth century, taking the great heartland regions of Africa as a whole, there was no decisive break in this expansion or decisive change in its nature. The early systems grew and spread and diversified in a thousand cultural contrasts. But progress came from the modification of what existed rather than from any departure in system or in structure. It came, in short, from growth rather than development. Much was taken from outside, not least by the influence of Islam; yet whatever was taken could also be absorbed, and therefore was absorbed, by the reform of structures and systems already in place.[4]

By the early or middle nineteenth century, however, this steady growth had begun to break through its containing institutions. Harried here and there by external factors of disintegration, such as the inland slave trade from the Zanzibari Coast, or the consequences of the much older and much larger Atlantic slave trade, the ancient checks and balances of traditional society began to give way to royal autocracies, to vast reorganizations of power, to a general increase of interstate rivalry and warfare. All this is hard to document precisely; yet one thinks of the careers of the nineteenth-century Buganda kings, so different from their predecessors; of the southern wars, from which the Zulu empire came, on a scale not known before; of the rise of new state bureaucracies in kingdoms such as Ashanti; of the later response to European invasion of men such as Samori Turay in the western Sudan; and of much else to the same effect. There is even a sense, perhaps, in which the present period of warlords is little more than a pendant to that other period of warlords, that nineteenth-century period, when the precedents and teachings of tradition had begun to seem no longer viable.

There were no new solutions then, though several were attempted;[5] instead, the Europeans came and assumed command of African history; and the solutions they found were solutions for themselves, not for Africans. This does not mean that Africans became the helpless objects of European control. On the contrary, much of colonial history reveals a profound and many-sided interaction between Europeans and Africans. Yet the Europeans were still in command. And they used this command to impose an institutionalized relationship between Africans and Europeans — between Africans and the capitalist systems that Europeans were then developing — of a specific and colonial nature. This included, true enough, a measure of development: one thinks of the introduction or enlargement of cash-crop economies; but not of a development which Africans could command. In that sense the colonial period imposed a standstill on African development, although not, of course, on African growth. At least in its later decades, the colonial period greatly deepened the crisis of growth that was already in play. Preventive medicine began to swell the size of populations at a rate not known before. And the dismantlement of traditional structures was confirmed, year by year, with the steady accumulation of slum-dwellers on the verge of cities, and the accompanying destruction of traditional custom and belief.

And so it was that the inherent crisis assumed tummultuous form in the last colonial years. With the pent-up force of growing problems, with the energies of multitudes of people suddenly released upon the scene, there came then the impression of a crisis that was new in kind as well as, certainly, new in scale. This impression was misleading, for it ignored too many of the facts of late precolonial and early colonial history. Yet so violent and all-consuming were the contesting forces now upon the stage that one could almost believe that Africans had been robbed of their birthright — of the chance to develop new institutions and systems of their own — even before they had come into possession of it: or that they regained command of their own history at a time, and under circumstances, which denied them any real hope of exercising that command.

To demonstrate the *fact* of crisis is therefore not difficult. "Nobody following an elephant," to borrow an Akan proverb collected by the Reverend J. G. Christaller almost a century ago, "needs to knock the dew off the grass." Yet there is still a large number of interesting questions that one can ask about this elephant and its line of march.

In approaching these questions, it may be well to emphasize that these last ten or fifteen years of political independence have by no means been altogether wasted: on the contrary, they have witnessed important gains. Not the least of these gains — and we shall have reason to note others as we go along — rests in a new clarity of thought about the realities of Africa's condition and predicament.

It is possible now, as it was barely possible before, to measure the extent of the damage brought about by a cumulative failure, over the past century and more, to meet these steadily emerging problems of growth with appropriate solutions: with the basic changes, whether social or economic or cultural, which are required in order to realize the potentials of African human and material resources. And if anyone were inclined to be pessimistic about Africa's future it is here that the justification would lie: for the circumstances of this long frustration of constructive change are now, beyond any doubt, extremely hard to deal with. And they are hard to deal with, let me repeat, precisely because they cannot now respond to any merely palliative or reformist relief.

There is, for instance, the connected question of population growth. For the first time in history, the Africans are now confronted by a great and growing imbalance between the rate of population growth and the physical means of supporting it.

A reasonable guess has suggested that the total population of the continent, outside the lower valley of the Nile, was perhaps three or four million at the onset of the African Iron Age, some 2,000 years ago. Another fairly reasonable guess proposes that these populations had increased to a total lying somewhere between 100 and 150 million by the beginning of the nineteenth century. They had expanded, in other words, in general balance with the means of their subsistence. And this is a view that is much confirmed by the historical evidence: there were never, so far as we know, any times of great and general famine such as are associated with populations grown far beyond their means of support.[6]

Another educated guess suggests that the rate of increase accelerated during the nineteenth century. If there were somewhat over 100 million in 1800, there may have been as many as 150 million by 1900. This would indicate a 50 percent increase over one hundred years:

already dangerously much within existing systems of production, and yet, for the most part, still absorbable by those systems.

But what happens then? The same run of guesses, better informed now, puts the total in 1960 at 273 million; and now, as we know, the rate soars upward in an entirely new progression. The total today is probably nearer 350 million. With an annual average growth rate in most countries of 2½ percent, and sometimes more, the prospect is of nearly 800 million by the year 2000. If most Africans are poor today, they are evidently going to be much poorer then: unless, of course, they can meanwhile achieve major changes in their systems of production and exchange.

Now a rate of increase, even of this magnitude, would in fact be a positive factor, at least for a while, under conditions of overall social and economic development. There is here no *general* case for Malthusian gloom; that applies only to the situation as we have it now. Much of Africa could undoubtedly support many more people if these people could liberate their own productive resources and capacities. In this respect, if no other, the crisis continues to be one of growth: the need for new systems and structures derives from the sheer buoyancy of African life. What an "optimum" total of people in Africa might be must remain an open question. But even in terms of market considerations, an Africa with a unified internal market, or a small number of unified regional markets, would probably call for *at least* four or five hundred million: in any case for far more people than are living there today.

Yet Africa, as things stand now, is very far from being

organized into a unified internal market, or even into a number of large regional markets. Not only that; most of its two score national markets defend their separateness with an eager determination. Many of these national markets number fewer than three million persons each, and have an overall economic product smaller than that of Glasgow or Detroit, Düsseldorf or Milan. There are a few comparative giants, but these, like the rest, labor under handicaps deriving from systems of low productivity.

It appears to be true that food production, to mention only that, is growing at an average rate which is decreasingly capable of feeding these populations even at their level of a dozen years ago. There is much to suggest that the average standard of everyday consumption, in many if not most of these countries, is lower than it was on the day of their political independence.

Could it have been otherwise? Here we reach a second chief indicator to the scale and nature of this crisis.

The economies which these countries inherited from the colonial period — whether in their domestic workings or in their relationship with oversea markets — were and are so structured as to constrict their systems of food production. Relatively rich or well-endowed countries, such as Ghana or Ivory Coast, were and still are geared to the export of farming crops: cocoa, coffee, peanuts, and the like. These are the export crops from which their producing countries have to live in the world market, the crops without which they would be labeled down and out. Yet the very growing of these crops cuts ever more deeply into their capacity to grow local food, diverts capital from food production, or tends to keep systems of food production in their traditional modes and methods.

It is a long time since Margaret Field observed of Ghana that "in spite of seasonal bursts of spending on luxuries, cocoa has lowered the basic standards of living and nutrition."[7] She was writing of the cocoa-growing areas. Where people can live — or even, given their options, must live — by growing crops for export, they do not grow crops for food, or they grow far less than they otherwise would. But the evidence for locally-grown-food shortage in rapidly expanding towns appears even more alarming.

And so an ever-increasing shortage of home-grown food has to be met by importing foreign food. More and more comes in with every year. Ghana's bill for foreign food was fifty-five million cedis in 1969, but seventy-nine million in 1970. Nigeria's was thirteen million Nigerian pounds for the first six months of 1970, but 19 million for the first six months of 1971; and you will find much the same picture elsewhere.

So a continent whose population is still more than 80 percent agrarian is spending a large and growing part of its meager annual revenues on buying food that it fails to produce for itself. In 1961 the overall African food import bill was estimated at some £150 million: today it must be considerably more than double that amount. Tomorrow — if it can be met — the bill for foreign food will be larger still. And when, in 1990, the population reaches some 700 million, as it will on present projections, most Africans will be eating foreign food or, one must greatly fear, will be scarcely eating at all; and as things are going now we may then expect to see, repeated in Africa, the same tale of famine or destitution told for so long about the Indian subcontinent.

A continent so organized as not to be able to feed from its own resources even its present 350 million will thus have to live on the world's charity, as well as buying foreign food with the annual surplus that it should be spending on its own development. This is a grim case, if ever there was one, of the eating of the seed corn.

It is sometimes argued that productive successes, here and there, make this view unreasonably pessimistic. Gross national products, we are told, can be and have been caused to expand at a sensational rate of growth. But we ought to know better, by this time, than to take such statistical abstractions as "gross national product" as any serious indicator of what is really going on. Gross domestic product may expand, even sensationally; it can still not mean development — or developmental change — in any serious sense.

Northern Rhodesia, which became Zambia in 1964, became a major source of copper after 1930. Its gross domestic product steadily expanded during the 1940s, positively boomed during the 1950s. In tropical African terms, Northern Rhodesia had something of the position of one of the larger oil sheikdoms of the Middle East. Yet in 1964, when the country became independent, some four-fifths of its population were still living and producing in exactly the same ways as before the copper boom, and at the same low levels of technology. Of the remaining fifth no longer living in the rural areas, only about 225,000 were listed as employed within the money economy. Even they were employed at artificially low rates of pay. As small a proportion as 12 percent of all

23

the workers in the money economy — in the wage-earning economy — received 50 percent of the total wages paid: almost all of these favored workers were immigrant whites whose savings, if they made any, generally went abroad.[8]

What this kind of boom really meant can be demonstrated by two facts. About half of the total capital surplus generated in the Northern Rhodesian economy was annually transferred abroad, mainly as copper-mining dividends. Secondly, in 1964 on the day of independence, Zambia inherited exactly one secondary school capable of carrying Africans to the level of the senior Cambridge certificate. So far as the bulk of the population was concerned, a soaring gross domestic product had about as much value as an avalanche of bowler hats.

But then, it may be said, these were colonial conditions. Since independence, African governments have been able to reduce the rate of dividend export, and begin the accumulation of capital for development, as well as greatly enlarging their social services. And many African governments have, of course, done these things, and at times with much success. They have begun to educate their peoples, cut down the flow of profits overseas, acquire possession or part-possession of their natural resources. Yet even the most effective of these governments is still enmeshed, through no fault of its own, in the constricting economic relationships taken over from the past. They remain dependent on world markets in which they have little or no say on prices; and the terms of trade have continued (with some exceptions) to move against them.

They remain, that is, primary producers whose low levels of productivity are set off against low levels of wage payment. Of upwards of forty countries with governments which, at least in theory, are sovereign, no fewer than eleven remain substantially dependent on the earnings of one major export product of a primary and unprocessed sort. A dozen more are substantially dependent on the earnings of two such export products, while all the others, though capable of offering three or more such products, occupy the same general posture.[9] Not only does this, as we have seen, adversely affect their capacity for growing food: it also continues the overall colonial relationship, and does so on price terms whose general trend is adverse to African interests.

But the explanation of why all this is so, and continues to be so, does not lie in the structure of world prices. These prices are effect rather than cause. The ever-widening gap in usable wealth between the populations of the so-called poor countries and those of the so-called rich countries has to be traced to factors which underlie the world price structure. These factors all trace back, in turn, to that international division of labor which reached maturity during the nineteenth century: the division, in terms of developing mechanical power and industrial wealth, between a handful of Western countries and the rest of the world, including Africa.

Long in preparation, with its origins in the history of Mediterranean society and its infancy in the great mercantile systems of eighteenth-century Britain and France, this was the international division that presided in the nineteenth century over the industrial revolutions of

Western Europe and North America, and, in large reflection of these profound systemic changes, over the imperialist subjection of Africa. Prolonged and further deepened during the twentieth century, this division has continued to widen the gap of inequality in power and usable wealth between the industrialized countries and their economic servants, the "primary producers."

In this process of deepening inequality, quite unchecked by the ending of direct imperialism, the adverse trend of prices has become of minor importance, and sometimes of none at all. What the "primary producers" suffer from now is not so much bad "terms of trade" — a relationship between import and export prices that is unfavorable to them — but, far more, their position of institutionalized subjection within the general economic system. The history of the last hundred and fifty years has so arranged matters that a deepening inequality in power and usable wealth has become endemic to the whole system, with more and more capital piling up at one end of it, and more and more poverty at the other.

This is true, of course, in every aspect of the system and to the point, so very obvious today, that increasing power and wealth *within* the rich countries can and evidently must go hand-in-hand with the increasing helplessness and deprivation of a vast quantity of more or less permanently unemployed workers. In the international sense, this spawning of poverty by wealth is still more obvious. On the one hand, you find a continual scientific and organizational feedback into industrial structures of rising productivity; on the other, you find a continued stagnation in the nonindustrial countries.

So it is that the poor have to run ever faster to stay even where they are; and still they fail.

One of the important analytical advances of the last few years has lain in a large amount of new discussion on the nature and "mechanics" of this whole process of deepening inequality, notably by economists in France, Britain, and the United States. They have examined the general orthodox theory of "development," whether by "foreign aid" or other means, and drawn attention to its illusions and ambiguities. They have looked at the actual condition of the "underdeveloped" countries, as well as that of the "developed," and have shown why "foreign aid," on balance and in present circumstances, is and can be no more than a contribution to that very process of deepening inequality which "foreign aid" is often supposed to reduce or even banish.[10]

The main point here is that "foreign aid" within the existing international system takes the general form not of a transfer of wealth, of capital, from "the rich" to "the poor," but of another installment in the export of investment capital by "the rich." Such "aid" may be palliative at certain points, helping to build this or that road or dam or deepwater harbor, and thus contributing to the physical infrastructure of the recipient country. But these contributions have to be paid for by a deepening indebtedness; their general effect, in any case, is to help towards increasing exports by the recipient country — in the nature of things, exports of "primary products" — and thus to reinforce the system, not to change it. The productivity of the whole system and relationship grow; they do not develop into a different system and relationship. And the major gains from this higher productivity continue, as before, to flow into the "developed" part of the system, making the latter once again comparatively stronger, more powerful, and with larger access to usable wealth. This is what Gunder Frank, and others after him, have called "the development of underdevelopment."

Some examples may be helpful here. Samir Amin, for example, has considered the situation of "unequal exchange" in relation to Senegal and other West African countries.[11] Thus the republic of Senegal has long been largely dependent upon the export of peanuts. So far as the figures show, the terms of trade have moved adversely against Senegal only to the extent of about 20 percent over the past fifty years: a steady rate of wealth-transfer overseas, and yet not a great one. But if one takes into account the relative increase of productivity of the French producer within *his* system, compared with the relative stagnation of the productivity of the Senegalese producer within his, the picture becomes a rather different one. The exchange relationship can then tell us a great deal more about the reasons why the gap in average living standards has never ceased to widen since the outright colonial period began.

In Senegal the quantity of labor contained in an export-unit of peanuts — apart, it seems, from some improvement in the transport element — is much the same as it was fifty years ago. Yet the quantity of labor contained in an export-unit of French textiles (or almost any other export item) has not remained the same. It has become steadily smaller, although, in spite of this, even the manifest terms of trade have just as steadily moved in favor not of Senegal but of France. Samir Amin suggests that this steady devaluation in the relative economic power of Senegalese labor may be of the order of seven times in terms of relevant prices. In other words, if the Senegalese producer were to have the same buying power in relation to French imports as he had in the 1880s, when the peanut economy was introduced, he would have to be paid about seven times more for his crops than he is paid today.

If I have dwelt at rather tedious length upon the economic arguments, it is because they dominate the scene. What a closer analysis will confirm, as I hope to show, is that the general system of relationships between African countries and their former rulers is in all essentials the same as it was during the outright colonial period, and that the roots of the present crisis lie precisely in this and in its implications.

The development of the industrialized countries continues to imply the stagnation — now, even, the regression — of the nonindustrialized. The strong continue to feed upon the weak; and the weak continue to grow weaker. And it is to this, far more than to anything else, that one must refer the troubles and upheavals — even, here and there, the downright banditries and piracies — of the newly independent regimes. Not until this system and relationship begin to be radically changed will there be, or can there be, any resolution of a crisis which threatens now to become catastrophe.

Can this system and relationship be changed? No doubt they can: not even the weak and powerless can be mocked for ever. But a more pointed question will meanwhile be: are there any present signs that they are being changed?

There are various claimants on the scene. Much is talked of the benevolent intentions of the developed world. Foreign aid, one often hears, is still going to be able to provide the answer. The rich will share with the poor, and the poor will grow rich. Yet even if that were really a possible solution, there is precious little evidence of its happening, as between whole societies and not mere privileged groups, on more than a token scale, and often not even on that. So much is seen, at an obvious level, in the failure of the Third World countries to secure a better price structure. Or it can be seen in the tendency of private investment to go into developed countries rather than underdeveloped ones. Or in the generally diminishing quantities of governmental aid. There are even strong reasons for believing that the total of foreign aid from the rich to the poor is smaller, on balance, than the total of wealth-transfer (whether by debt service, dividends, or other means) going from the poor to the rich. Africans, in any case, have little reason to feel hopeful about foreign aid. In a world context, their share of such aid, over the years 1960–1967, dwindled from about 35 percent to about 23 percent: in the very years, that is, when they have needed it most. More than that, it further appears that the net real transfer of other resources from the industrialized countries to Africa also fell during this period, and has since continued to fall. On the other side of the balance, meanwhile, there is not the slightest doubt that African payments to the industrialized countries, whether in debt service or other transfers, have generally climbed throughout these years, and are still climbing today.

Within the existing structures or relationships, one may repeat, foreign aid can be at best no more than palliative; and what is palliative will not now save the day. Foreign aid designed to improve "what exists" may ease a little the shoe that pinches; the shoe will still be far too small.[12] And it may not even ease the shoe but make it smaller still. If that sounds paradoxical, consider the startling and major case of the Republic of South Africa.

All through the 1960s it was above all to South Africa, or rather to the white-dominated sector of South Africa's economy, that the rich countries' investments went. At any rate after 1961 and the shock of the Sharpeville massacre of Africans by police bullets, development capital has been flowing into South Africa at a rate so large as to have increased that economy's net capital formation by a regular 5 percent a year. With this expansion, white South Africa today has ceased to be a colonial economy, a mere branch of the British and other capitalist systems in Europe and North America, and has become a system on its own. Here, if nowhere else, it has proved possible to erect a genuine, because self-generating, capitalist structure in Africa.[13]

But what does this do for Africans? Inside the Republic, there are some "spread effects" which are shared by a proportion of urbanized Africans. But these benefits are small and do not reach the rural multitudes. On the contrary, the rural multitudes become poorer through this process of urban-industrial expansion; the shoe becomes steadily smaller, and pinches continually harder.[14]

Meanwhile the liberalizing of the apartheid system, so often forecast as an "inevitable" consequence of economic expansion, has entirely failed to appear. Far from that, we have seen that with every fresh expansion the screws of racist discrimination have been turned a little harder, and sometimes more than a little. In a caste economy, it is evidently just as possible to have prosperity and privilege for the few coupled organically with continued and deepening oppression for the many, as it is, in our class economies, to have what the economists have always told us was impossible: mass unemployment coupled with inflation, or what is now known as "stagflation."

This is why the payment of higher wages to African workers in South African industries will not "liberalize" the apartheid system, but rather will serve to reinforce the whole system of racist discrimination by easing some of its strains. Obviously it is a good thing in itself to improve the level of African wages from their present starvation or near-starvation levels. But it remains at best a self-delusion to suppose that any such improvement will change the system. It will merely raise the absolute levels of wages, while the relative levels remain where they were before. The detailed evidence to this effect is both complete and conclusive.[15]

The conclusion has to be the same about another related argument: that white South African agreement to the entry of black workers into skilled industrial employment will similarly "liberalize" the system, and gradually destroy apartheid. Nothing, as things stand today, seems less likely. The apartheid system is perfectly capable of absorbing skilled black labor, while still maintaining its racist discrimination against non-whites. Indeed, what the apartheid system now requires, with the development of its self-generating capitalist economy, is precisely the transformation of unskilled or semiskilled labor into skilled labor. All that happens, then, is that the color bars are raised once again, as often in the past half century. The apparatus of discrimination stays intact, operating at a relatively higher level of industrial skills. The Africans remain subject to all the pains and penalties of racist law; the only difference is that some of them, in the cities, receive a little more money and eat a little less badly. The change, as one can see, works for the system rather than against it. Any genuine liberalization is as far away as ever, and perhaps even farther, if only because the system emerges stronger than before. Its white beneficiaries acquire more usable wealth and hence more usable power.

More important in a general sense, what does this development of the Republic of South Africa by foreign aid do for Africans outside that unhappy country's borders? Here we meet another illustration of the damage that is done by the existing system of relationships. For huge quantities of the rich world's money are now invested in a South Africa that is eager, by the sheer impulsion of its own development, to expand its influence. Ten years ago the late Prime Minister Hendrik Verwoerd canvassed the idea of a Southern African Common Market which the Republic would lead and dominate. And much has been done by successive governments to try to realize that aim. Understandably enough: the Republic today is a country with booming export industries and capital to place abroad. What more natural than to seek to build, with African countries, the same kind of relationship with those countries, whether colonial or postcolonial, that Britain and France have enjoyed and still enjoy?

And so we see, even at this late stage, a new chapter of imperialism being written. Whether the chapter will be completed is another question; the opening pages, at least, are already there. And they are there, in large part, thanks to what is called foreign aid. What they point towards is something like a planetary system with satellites. Within the general area of South Africa, Lesotho and Botswana and Swaziland along with sundry little "Bantustans," such as the Transkei and Zululand, are to revolve around the Sun of Pretoria. Further away, but still obediently revolving, there are to be other satellites of varying kinds: Malawi for one, perhaps Angola and Mozambique, if possible Zambia, even the whole area of the Congo Basin.

It would be interesting to speculate on what may or may not befall such plans. But the point I wish to make here is that the South African case, however easily deplorable from an African standpoint, however extreme or eccentric, is in fact an integral and inseparable part of a much wider problem.

What the men of Pretoria are now trying to do is no way different in its essence, no matter how different it may be in some of its flavors and appearances, from what the imperialist countries did, there and elsewhere on the continent, seventy years ago and more. What these men are seeking to achieve, over the years ahead, is no different in kind from the achievement of the imperialist countries. In some respects they are not even out of date, for they have well learned the neocolonial lesson that economic hegemony need have no quarrel with the trappings of political self-rule.

Their hope, as they have been careful to express it, is to erect between themselves and as many African countries as possible a system of relationships which, whatever degree of formal or even real sovereignty it may afford to these countries, must subject them, and continue to subject them, to the prior and dominant needs of the South African system and its foreign investors.

Whatever agreeable title may be found, the essential relationship is to be imperialist. To the extent that this takes shape, the problems of constructive change can only be enlarged wherever this relationship prevails. And these problems can only be enlarged because this budding system, like its larger exemplars and partners elsewhere, rests and is intended to rest upon a steady transfer of wealth from the poor to the rich.

If this small survey has so far touched on factors bleakly negative, this is not because there is none more hopeful to be found. But the wind of an easy optimism will not take us very far. To find these positive factors, one needs to look at the situation as it really is, and to find out why it is as it is, and then, building on that, to consider how it may be changed and who, if anyone, is trying to change it. Let us then persevere with this analysis, first in the political field and then, in so far as one can sensibly separate the two, in that of economics.

CHAPTER TWO

The Heritage of Politics

Modern Africa is as much the child of its own past as any other part of the world. Reaching back through countless centuries, it is the product of African history, including, more recently, the processes of action and reaction set going by European contact, commerce, invasion, dispossession, and political withdrawal. All these factors form what may be called the "inherited situation." Here I am going to look at this situation from a mainly political standpoint.

Now in analyzing this inheritance, this framework of inherited problems within which, and often against which, independent politics have had to operate, one can usefully isolate *three controlling political factors.* These consist of the consequences of European imperialist policy, remote or recent; secondly, of the continuing influence of indigenous policy, expressed by "traditional" authorities taking their stand on African ideas and loyalties; and, thirdly, of the growing if often divergent impact of groups, movements, or parties inspired by modern ideas of nationalism. It will not be a gross oversimplification to interpret the complex drama of late-colonial and postcolonial Africa as an interplay between these factors, now with one of them dominant and now with another, in an often bewildering sequence of alliances and oppositions which change and shift and change again.

The inherited framework of this interplay, as one sees repeatedly, was and is stubbornly colonial. For proof of that, one need look no further than to the frontiers of today and the ideas of reformist nationalism. They form a large part of the inherited problem, but they come by way of European precept and example.

The Africa of a century ago consisted of several hundred independent states. Some of them were large and powerful, the outcome of a long process of structural growth within institutions which had undergone repeated modification and reform. Others were small in size or strength, little different in their structure from the patterns of an earlier day. Some of them had all the attributes of centralized government, of common language or at least a dominant language, of the sense of mutual loyalty and fate among their citizens, such as Europeans have associated with nationhood. Others had less of these qualities, and were bound together, within themselves, by little more than remote or occasional ties, often operative only when these communities were threatened from outside.

Today, by contrast, these several hundred states have become compressed into about forty units which are spoken of as nations, and whose policies are predicated on that basis. This condensation was not altogether irrational. But its rationality, in so far as any existed, derived not from African but from European ideas and interests.

Sometimes, true enough, the inter-European bargains which produced these frontiers were concerned with the winning of local advantages: just as often, they were concerned with nothing of the kind. One can only reflect with a wry astonishment at the historical oddity of some of those bargains. If the British had given up The Gambia to the French, as was proposed to them in the 1870s, they might have gained the Ivory Coast and more besides: in terms of local advantage they would have done themselves a great deal of good. But the British would not give up The Gambia, for reasons of English nationalism in England: on the good old grounds, that is, of "what we have, we hold."[1]

A little later the Sultan of Zanzibar offered Britain suzerainty over the whole of his coastal sphere of influence or occupation. But the British would only take the northern half of it, in spite of any question of local advantage, because it was thought preferable, for the benefit of British interests in the European "balance of power," to placate Bismarck by making over the southern half to Germany. If Portugal was able to gain a European preference over territories in Africa some twenty-two times larger than itself, this again had little to do with pressures or policies arising from questions of local advantage. But it had much to do with London's wish to use its little ally in Lisbon as an instrument for reducing the colonial influences of London's powerful rivals, especially those of Paris. As for King Leopold of Belgium, he acquired the greater part of the Congo Basin with only the vaguest ideas about its topography, and no idea at all about the interests of the peoples who were living there. He got it largely because he had powerful

European friends who wanted to annoy their similarly powerful European enemies.[2]

For a long time these lines on the map meant even less to the Africans thus enclosed. Frontier peoples, often nationally divided in this way, paid little regard to boundaries which made no sense. They crossed and recrossed them as they chose, stepping aside only when threatened by one or other of the innumerable "punitive expeditions" which carried out the long and weary process known rather oddly as pacification. Within the colonies thus established, traditional authorities made whatever bargains they were able, so as to conserve however much they could. The greater part of the history of the colonial period is composed of the record of what they did, or tried to do, and of how the colonial authorities behaved in response. This was the interplay which produced the diversities of colonial policy and law. What often came to seem, from the outside, a neat and regular system of British ideas, or French ideas, or of some other European ideas duly composed in colonial ministries, applied by colonial governors, and crowned with portentous titles such as "Indirect Rule" or "Dual Mandate" or whatever, was really nothing of the kind, but, in large part, a piecemeal response to African action and initiative.

The frontiers gradually took shape in African consciousness as well as on the map, and then in African acceptance, though always by an uneasy symbiosis of colonialist and traditionalist patterns of thought, and with a persistent undertone of African dissent. But then, however inappropriate to African interests they might be, these frontiers became the necessary framework of a new politics, the politics of anticolonial struggle: in the event, and with no alternative, the politics of a nationalism couched in European ideas and language. With no alternative, because, as things were then, anticolonial struggle could be led with any hope of success only by men educated in Europe and capable of using the political language and ideas of Europe.

Some of their early spokesmen — in West Africa, for example, those "morning stars" of independence who were the Blydens and Hortons and the Caseley Hayfords — might see the future in wider terms, and look to unities that would be larger than the divisive compartments, often the absurdly small compartments, of colonial rule. But colonial policy could not be interested in dreams of unity; and at no significant point in the record do you find — whether in the British record or any other — the slightest willingness to discuss any large redrawing of frontiers as part of the process of African advancement.

So it came about that even the wisest of the new politicians and thinkers of the mature colonial period were obliged to accept, and try to act within, but only within, the given colonial framework. To many of them, perhaps to most, this was of course the framework within which their whole formation tended to persuade them that they *ought* to act. They might well be the prophets of a different future; the revelations they had received were European, and these were the nationalist realities of Europe. Even the most perceptive of them were obliged to mold their thought by the realities they knew. Even the radical exceptions — from men such as Louis Hunkanrin in the 1920s[3] through the later colonial decades to men such as Azikiwe and Nkrumah, influenced as these often were by the unifying ideas of the Pan-Africanist movement — found it impossible, in practice, to act outside the framework of a consciously separatist nationalism. Jomo Kenyatta had been one of the stars of the last of the Pan-Africanist congresses; yet upon achieving power he at once felt it necessary to defend the semidesert northern territory of Kenya, occupied though it considerably was by peoples linked to Somalia, as an inalienable and sacred fragment of Kenya's national soil.

Thus the ideological situation at the time of independence was a curious fabric of conflicting interests and compromises. Hopeful outsiders might sit back and say on that auspicious day: behold, this or that nation is launched upon its modernizing path, and all the institutions that it needs are properly in place, awaiting only their due harvest of progress and development. To those inside, it seemed at best a difficult and tentative beginning, and down a road which they had only partly chosen, or had not chosen at all.

The ambiguities are clearer now. The educated élites would fill the ministries and parliaments as smartly as they could. But they would rule, in fact, according to the patterns of power which traditional politics had managed to safeguard. Or, if they would not do that, they would find themselves at once in strife and protest. Small wonder, perhaps, that few of the solemn ceremonials which attended the hauling down of colonial flags and the raising of national standards were greeted with much popular acclaim. To the man in the street, all too often, this tended to look like another arrangement of power to the advantage of those who were, already, the beneficiaries of colonial rule. Everyone loves a festival, and independence certainly induced a brief euphoria here and there, as well as a rapid and sensible calculation of possible immediate gains; but it set going no great cementing of new unities, and often it produced a sharp foreboding.

The uncertain note struck in those early days of independence, a dozen years ago and more, seems less puzzling in retrospect than it often did then. There were moments when it could seem very puzzling. On Nigeria's day of independence, late in 1960, the customary pomp and circumstance were unfolded in the customary sports arena. There were the customary fireworks, and the customary tribal dances, for civil service imagination seldom managed to allow itself to get beyond them; and then, climax to the grand occasion as the tropical night descended and the floodlights flared, the customary striking of the Union Jack and the raising of the new flag to the throb and call of appropriate drum and bugle voluntaries. Normally, this would be followed by a show of trick motor-cycling by the colonial police who, overnight, had now become the national police: a more or less gentle way, one always supposed, of making a point about continued law and order, and all that.

The civil service devisers of the Nigerian ceremony, having so large a country to launch upon its sovereign path, had thought of something on an altogether more emphatic scale. The Union Jack came down and the Nigerian flag went up, floodlit in their momentary silence. And then, as I recall, pandemonium exploded. There burst upon the dark arena, without one word of warning, a phalanx of armored cars firing blank ammunition at the assembled multitudes who thronged the encircling stands. This dreadful assault was brief and nobody was hurt, unless in the eardrums; but it was menacing. And whatever the devisers of that interlude may or may not have intended by it, the effect conveyed was unmistakable: days of wrath lay all too probably ahead.

The wrath, in fact, had scarcely begun. It was easy, then and for some while after, to overlook its probable dimensions; and all the more because there was undoubtedly a certain uplifting of hearts. For a little while, at least, it really seemed as though the simple act of scaling colonial bastions, the mere assertion of independence after such long denial in a world where Africans had suffered the slings and arrows of contempt, would be enough to solve all problems. It was as though this huge segment of humanity in Africa had acquired overnight the keys of self-discovery in the modern world; and this, by itself, might change everything.

And self-discovery did change much. Even today, historically close to those moments though we still are, it is already difficult to recall and recapture the colonial atmosphere, the deep provincial silence of imperial administration and its consequences on the public scene. But if one tries, then it is likely that not even the worst excesses of official pomp and privilege today will seem half as bad or as boring as the petty miseries of that time.

Back in 1954 I remember asking the chief of the native affairs department in Léopoldville, capital of the Belgian Congo,[4] for an opportunity to meet some educated Africans, some of those whom the Belgians called *évolués.* There was no other way of meeting *évolués* without being likely to involve them in awkward visits by the police. The request was granted in a manner that must now seem grotesque, but appeared perfectly normal then, and, at least to the administrators concerned, perfectly reasonable. A dozen educated Africans were duly bidden to attend a classroom in the native quarter, the *cité indigène,* and offered children's chairs in the body of the room, while the visitor, flanked by two Belgian officials, was given the liberty and privilege of asking questions across the teacher's table. The results, as you might expect, were meager. After such a situation, the coming of independence was like the stumbling from night into day. It was not the millennium of the prophets; yet there were moments, briefly and glitteringly, when it almost seemed that it might be.

Thinking back, wiser than before, one is above all impressed by the haphazardness of the whole process of decolonization. General histories written in the future may compress that process into a few neat pages and stages, suggesting some kind of logical and even long-planned order of events; they will be sadly astray. If the newly formed élites, the sudden inheritors of power, were opportunist, shifting as they could from one position of advance to another, abandoning one argument to urge a quite different one, leaping from one small gain to the next, so too, in a reverse sense, were the colonial powers. They, on their side, threw up emergency obstacles to this or that African initiative, sought to win time, fell back on abrupt acts of anger and oppression, enunciated constitutional programs of standstill or of limited gain, only to deny themselves almost before the ink was dry.

All the same, even in the most confused of colonial policies, there remained a certain underlying constancy of trend and concept, a certain persisting range of ideas about what should be allowed to happen, or, now and then, helped to happen. This range of ideas was not a new one: its origins had emerged even at the early stages of the colonial experience, when dispossession of Africans had been justified, in so far as justification seemed needful or desirable, by the vision of a civilizing mission. It rested in a series of nineteenth-century convictions about the nature of Africans and their cultures, the core of which was that these held within themselves no developmental virtue. If Africans were to move ahead, non-Africans would have to lead them and show them how. It was argued in countless solemn books and state papers that Africans needed to be given English institutions, or French or Belgian institutions, or even, however unpromising that may seem, Portuguese institutions. Endowed with these, they would be beneficially incorporated within the systems of the imperial motherlands until, at some remote and barely thinkable moment in the future, they might possibly be able to manage for themselves. Otherwise, it was said with much sad shaking of heads, there was simply no hope for them.

So it was that the framework emerged: by the defensive tactics of traditional authorities; by the effort of educated Africans who grasped whatever opportunities they could find of mastering the stratagems of nationalist Europe; and also, if in greatly varying form, by the more or less conscious shaping of the colonial powers. This process of colonial shaping became clearer as the pressures for change grew in strength.

Back in the 1930s it had mainly been a question of training suitable intermediaries: of selecting, for the most part, persons of traditional authority who would use this authority, directly or indirectly, to transmit colonial requirements and thus "carry along the masses without social disorder."[5] Where there were no identifiable chiefs, efforts were made to create them: such efforts often ended in frustration, but they were none the less persisted with. Where strong traditional authorities existed, it was much easier. Northern Nigeria was one region in which the policy could be easily applied; the French Sudan (Mali today) was another. An administrator of the Sudan, the Guyanese Félix Eboué, afterwards governor-general of the French Equatorial colonies during the Second World War, was one of those who explained the process. Of the early 1930s in the Sudan, he wrote that "in order to raise the intellectual level of chiefs, we undertook a judicious choice of children to admit in the schools, so that those destined by their origins to become chiefs should be among them": in 1933–1934, out of a total of 12,000 schoolchildren in the Sudan, no fewer than 1,500 were the sons of chiefs.[6]

Later on, with the rise of a nationalism which threatened to overtake and set aside the patterns of traditional authority, the choosing of intermediaries had to acquire a wider social context; often at this point in time, at least in West Africa, the intermediaries were able to choose themselves. Yet their only way of mastering the stratagems of European nationalism, and so of adding these to the stratagems of African tradition, was to pass through European schools and universities; and this, in turn, provoked imperial authority to an increasingly conscious effort at suitable indoctrination.[7]

By now, one needs to recall as well, all this was happening in the wake of a Second World War which had led, almost at once, to what was then known as the Cold War. In the colonial context, this produced an aggressive effort by the possessing powers to repel every idea which could be seen as the fruit of leftwing thought; and leftwing thought, for most of the administrators of those days, was in practice tantamount, at least in my experience, to any thought which questioned the wisdom of established orthodoxies.[8] Out of this there came another peculiar characteristic of the decolonizing process: though ostensibly preparing the way for a quite different future, it contained within itself a powerful aversion from considering what that future might be or should be.

In those years a visitor could meet a leading nationalist in the morning only to find an outraged policeman on his doorstep in the afternoon, threatening expulsion from the territory,[9] while any energetic student in Europe who had imbibed distrust of accepted verities was soon confronted, upon returning home, with a choice between shutting up or unemployment. When independence came, it was almost invariably through the filter of a thoroughly effective exclusion of all possible alternatives to the given framework. By no means everyone, of course, was fooled. The framework was accepted with acclamation by men who often knew that they were only playing out an allotted role, and that the measure of their skill in acting this part, in going through the motions, was also the measure of the speed with which the necessary constitutional concessions would be granted by Westminster or the Palais Bourbon.

Not only that. These given frameworks, these bourgeois-parliamentary models, were embedded by now in a doctrine, an official guide to policy, which had also acquired a certain coherence. One sees this most clearly in some of the great state papers of those years. None is more illuminating than the report of a Royal Commission which inquired, in 1953–1955, into the affairs of British East Africa: Kenya, Uganda, Tanganyika, Zanzibar. This report is memorable both for what it says and for what it fails to say. Its distinguished authors saw very well that things must change; that much was intolerable for any kind of civilized life for Africans, or even for African survival; that many policies were out of date if not utterly deplorable; and they listed these with the cool impartiality of metropolitan paternalism at its most cutting. But how should things be changed, and in what direction? "Much depends," they wrote, "on the emergence of a responsible African middle class who can meet members of other races on equal terms. . . . The first duty of government is to create the conditions which make development of a community of this kind possible."

It was the big theme of those years. Let us create, they urged, a middle class, so that this middle class can meet us on our own ground, and bridge the gulf between ourselves and them, the darkly threatening plebs of native Africa. Official policies said it. Well-meaning politicians echoed it. Christian dignitaries gave it their approval. Even as late as 1971, even in the embattled colony of

Angola, a pastoral letter of Portuguese bishops was still saying it. "What is absolutely necessary," they advised, "is that we build an African middle class . . . for only in this way can we fulfill our mission and justify the laws which we obey."

But what the bishops did not say, any more than the Royal Commissioners had said, or any other exponent of the "middle-class solution," was what they meant by an "African middle class." I think they would have told you, had you asked, that they meant all that kind of Africans who were clerks and plumbers and truck drivers, petty traders, primary schoolmasters, people who were beginning to live in towns above the hunger line, and even to enjoy a little material comfort.

Another Belgian Congo memory of 1954 comes back to me: of discussing this very point with an administrator who, pressed for an example, took me down to the *cité indigène* and into the small house of an African whose bedroom duly revealed to us his possession of no fewer than twenty pairs of shoes. What better proof of middle-class status?

But if you went a little further, and asked whether this middle class with all its pairs of shoes was destined, in the official mind, to become an investing class, a capitalist class, then you would be likely to receive either a patient smile of pity for your ignorance, or a request to keep your politics to yourself. Such questions were unpleasing, for they were bound, if answered, to lay bare the intellectual poverty of the official "plan." Besides, they invited other questions. How could one imagine a parliamentary democracy without capitalists: that is, local capitalists, African capitalists? But in what way were such capitalists to be produced within the colonial framework?

They were terribly obvious questions, but you will read the great state papers in vain for any answers. For what the colonial powers evidently wished to promote was no genuine kind of middle class, but convenient tools or intermediaries.

There lay at the heart of colonial policy, accordingly, a large and immovable equivocation wherever any question of a different future was concerned. And it is the confusions of this equivocation, compounded through the years, that one sees on every side today, whether in African situations or in non-African opinions about those situations.

On one hand the colonial powers preached the advent of democracy on parliamentary models: making an African capacity to work such models a main criterion of "progress achieved"; installing national assemblies in buildings modeled on the House of Commons or the Palais Bourbon; equipping these with libraries of rule and precedent drawn from European experience in Europe, with staffs and wigs and all the jargon of parliamentary pomp and *politesse:* just as though, at the waving of a Speaker's mace or some other act of sympathetic magic, the whole processive development of European history was to be encapsulated and installed within the quite different history of Africa.

Or they contrived electoral and other laws of representation of a positively cabalistic complexity, of which those elaborated for British Central Africa were perhaps the most remarkable in their arithmetical flights of calculation about "A" rolls and "B" rolls and small-print reservations of this and that. As late as 1971 there came another of these miasmic formulas in proposals under which Rhodesian Africans were to accede to majority rule in fifty-five years, or perhaps five hundred and fifty-five. Such absurdities were duly launched upon a baffled electorate with many dreadful warnings of what must befall if the most perfect democracy should fail thereafter to appear.

From another angle, but far more vaguely, official policies predicated the building of capitalist systems, though actual use of the word "capitalist" was generally frowned on as being somehow subversive. These were to be systems in which African "middle classes," as the East Africa Royal Commissioners had put it, could meet members of other races "on equal terms": on the terms, that is, of middle-class white society. Such systems, it was said in learned papers intended to be taken seriously, could be the sole guarantee of peace, stability, and progress for the many as well as for the few. The evidence of Europe itself might be bleakly to the contrary: never mind, such systems alone could meet the requirements of parliamentary democracy, and parliamentary democracy was the *sine qua non* of civilization. The rest could only be a problem for the police.

It will be charitable to think that these policy makers had forgotten Europe's history. Their own capitalist systems, they would otherwise have known, had not emerged and grown strong under any conditions of democracy recognizable today. They had in fact become mature during a long period of harsh minority rule, or, putting it less politely, of an oligarchical dictatorship modified, now and then, by recourse to a corrupted ballot-box. An interesting parallel has been drawn between the corruptions and coercions of eighteenth-century England and twentieth-century Nigeria, and it could certainly be extended, both in time and place.[10] Yet the parallel arises not from any particular venality of the peoples in question, even of the English, but from parallel efforts at building capitalist systems. The one, like the other, took the only possible means of making middle classes grow and prosper to the point at which they can exercise hegemony: that is, by the despoilment of others in the state; while not forgetting, of course, that in due time the poachers will turn gamekeepers, and wax in wrath at any least attack upon the sacred rights of property. Nothing, historically, could be less well founded than the reproaches offered by the modern gamekeepers of Europe and America to the modern poachers of Africa: the latter, after all, are only doing their best to become like the former.

Built into the starting situation, in other words, was a major contradiction between the enunciated ends of policy and the proposed means of reaching those ends. Either the Africans could embrace the ideals of democracy and give up trying to form middle classes, or they could do the reverse; they could certainly not do both. It has taken them a little time to understand these traps into which they have been led, or have walked of their own accord.

If, then, the persistence of backward-looking traditional authorities and of self-regarding élites with middle-class aspirations were part of the inherited problem, the guiding hand of the colonial powers formed a still greater

52

part. What emerged, through the push and pull of these formative factors, was the nationalist pattern of today with all its inadequacy and inherent provocation of strife. But there again, looking at this pattern of reformist nationalism in its present helplessness, one is repeatedly struck by colonial responsibility for its divisiveness. The fission of the French colonial federations into a scatter of states, each with few inhabitants, is a case that comes to mind.

For most of the late colonial period the eight territories of French West Africa (nine with Togo, a United Nations "Trusteeship Territory") were governed from Dakar as little more than subordinate provinces of a single administration, just as the four of Equatorial Africa (five with Cameroun, another "Trusteeship Territory") were governed from Brazzaville. When the liberated French Republic, after 1945, offered an entry to the National Assembly of deputies from Africa, some of these came from the interterritorial Rassemblement Démocratique Africain (RDA). And for a little while there were no few leaders, among the new deputies, who thought that colonial federation should be made into independent federation. "The real solution of our problem," declared one of the best known of them, Léopold Senghor, in 1954, "is federation," though it is true that he also had in mind that this should be federation with France.[11] Others went far beyond. "We see French West Africa," another remarked as late as 1959, when any such hope had become exceedingly remote, "surmounting both colonialism and its own petty loyalties of tribalism, and emerging as a great and sovereign federation. I go much further than that," he went on: "My own deep hope is that we are moving toward the federal unity of the whole of West Africa."[12] Apocalyptic vision, no doubt; yet it stood for an idea that was really there. Only a year earlier the constitution of an independent Guinea had declared that "the Republic may conclude agreements for association or community with any African state, going as far as partial or total abandonment of sovereignty, in order to realize the unity of Africa." And other constitutions were soon to say much the same.

Vain words, as we know. They offered a supranationalist destiny to a nationalist horse that was determined, by now, to stay where it was; and for powerfully persuasive reasons. The early efforts of the RDA had been met with great administrative resistance; on the eve of the 1950s, even with stiff repression. And when concessions were at last agreed upon, they put the accent strongly on territorial independence at the cost of any kind of supraterritorial organs of self-rule. True enough, within what was now called the French Union, the decisive concession of 1956 — the so-called framework law, or *loi cadre* — reserved defense, foreign affairs, and finance to the still colonial federal authority in Dakar. Yet it handed useful though lesser powers to territorial councils of ministers: the lesson for the nationalists could not have been more obvious. If they wished to exploit this concession in order to obtain others, they must do it on the basis of territorial separatism. The often absurd frontiers of West African colonialism were to acquire the sanctity of national pride and honor.[13]

The point was driven home as early as August of the same year, 1956. Togo was elevated to the status of an autonomous republic within the French Union: not yet fully sovereign, yet halfway towards becoming so. With fewer than two million inhabitants, this Togo was in fact only the eastern two-thirds of the original German colony, the remainder being in British hands. Yet these two-thirds were endowed with the attributes of approaching nationhood as though this must be their manifest and separate destiny. With that and with what followed, the modern "balkanization" of this vast West African region colonized by France could only be a matter of time.

What followed was that de Gaulle, in 1958, offered his famous referendum. The voters of these colonies could choose between a separatist independence of each country on its own, or continued membership of what was now called, still more equivocally, the French Community. Many of the dominant territorial parties probably or certainly wished by now for the first alternative, as being the only way of progress that was open to them: against furious French opposition, Guinea alone was able to achieve it.[14] But with Guinea's separate independence at the end of 1958, the chips were down. Hopes of an independent federal reorganization, of welding all these populations into an organic cooperation which would still give room for local diversity and loyalty, were at an end.

Yet the process of "balkanization" was by no means at an end. A nationalism of this type and content, taking over the heritage of traditionalist separatism and modernist élitism, lost little time in producing its natural son and heir, micronationalism, or, as observers soon began calling it, "tribal nationalism."

If dominant groups in Colony A were convinced that they, and therefore Colony A, could do better on their

55

own than in unity or federation with Colony B and Colony C, then other groups, down the scale, could draw the same conclusion. Thus, in any given country, the dominant group of People A could and soon did argue that they too might do better on their own rather than in unity with People B and People C; and separatist pressures often became the rule.

Here one needs to distinguish. Some measure of "tribal nationalism" must have emerged in any case, for in one large and important sense this was and is the expression of genuine cultural differences formed over a very long period of time. Such differences and the local loyalties which they promote must evidently call for a progressive devolution to local autonomy; and this, for example, is the intention of the twelve-state constitution of Nigeria today. The trouble with the "tribal nationalism" of the early decolonizing years was that it encouraged this or that "leading group" against rival groups, whether traditionalist or "middle class," in ways that were bound to be, and duly became, reactionary and regressive.

Colonial prejudice or policy was certainly much to blame. But here again there was equivocation. On one side, colonial spokesmen said that they deplored "tribal nationalism," and often enough, with tears of paternal anguish in their eyes, adduced this as an excuse for slowing the process of primary decolonization. On the other side, colonial policy generally acted to protect, buttress, and even enhance the position of those very groups, the bearers of this micronationalism, in whom it saw its most reliable "partners." As with the parallel policy of building-a-middle-class, whatever might be proclaimed as colonial theory was regularly denied or frustrated by

56

colonial practice. This, too, was part of the heritage of confusion into which an independent Africa had to step.

There were those who marked this divisive trend, and thought it a recipe for trouble. "While it is claimed that the effect of British policy [in West Africa] is to provide a framework which holds the national groups together," remarked a British critic in 1953, "it could equally well be argued that it creates a situation in which the maximum encouragement is given to tribal nationalism, and any political adventurer who proclaims himself a champion of the natural rights of the Yorubas, Ibos, or northerners can expect to succeed."[15] Of the acutely divisive structure then taking shape in colonial Nigeria, the same critic likewise observed: "The basic principle underlying the present three-region system of government is that Nigeria consists of three nations, and that each nation must be prevented [by an impartial British administration] from encroaching upon the rights and interests of the other two. In this way British power becomes itself a cause of divisions, and throws its weight on the side of the forces of particularism against those making for Nigerian unity."[16]

Elsewhere, the divisive role of colonial policy was clearer still. The people of Kenya, early in the 1960s, were obliged by colonial policy to promote their national unity with a constitution which gave great emphasis to tribal nationalism. This constitution provided for a central legislature, but it also provided for seven regional legislatures, each of which was to have its own government and civil service, its own judiciary and police force, its own border controls and other public bodies. That this recipe for the balkanization of Kenya was rapidly superseded by a strongly centralizing constitution is not the point here: the point is that the framework devised by colonial policy was deliberately destructive of any organic unification. The wider unities which could alone offer a road to stability and social expansion were to be sacrificed for the benefit of sectionalist interests, élitist interests: in this case, above all, for the benefit of a white minority concentrated in the central highlands, and anxious to save what it could from the wreck of its own hopes of exercising a Kenya-wide hegemony.

Willingly or not, the élites played out their appointed roles: some with reluctance, others with enthusiasm, nearly all of them with style and skill. Duly presented with a framework which favored an élitist type of growth, they took over power. Many of them continued to perform their appointed roles, and set about the task of dividing up the immediate spoils of independence so as to use these for their own enrichment. And how otherwise, than by accumulating wealth at the direct expense of their fellow countrymen, could they hope to build themselves into a bourgeoisie, into a genuine middle class able to launch and dominate a new capitalist system? This was what colonial policy had said that they should do. But when they did it they were much blamed by their mentors in Europe. These had long since become gamekeepers of eminent respectability, and wagged their fingers at this reckless poachers' enterprise. But when other kinds of leadership turned to other means of progress, as in Guinea or Ghana, the gamekeepers stopped wagging their fingers and started shaking their fists.

The voters, not too surprisingly, could take a different

view. More and more, they have objected to an independence which has often seemed no more than a change of masters. As they have protested, so have the tumults grown. And with growing tumult, the civil wing of ruling groups have looked for means of self-defense and found it, or sometimes had it found for them, in their armies and army officers. Then the underlying equivocation breaks into the light of day: either the ideas of an egalitarian democracy must go to the wall, or ruling groups must abdicate their power. All too understandably, in the present stage of transition, democracy becomes the victim. Yet this is not to say that the ambitions of such groups, even with the aid of military protectors, can expect to avoid frustration. As I expect to be able to show in due course, this "solution," this attempt to build genuine because self-generating capitalist systems based on native capitalist classes, will not in any case succeed, no matter how energetically it may be attempted.

The process of frustration, perhaps needless to say, has not been simple nor is it now conclusive: the story will continue for a long while yet. But this is where the essence of most of Africa's problems may be confidently said to rest. It lies in the persistence of the inherited structure: in the roles given to traditionalist groups, in the emergence of élites modeled on a "middle-class solution," and, promoting and orchestrating these, in the resolutely conservative character of Western policy and influence, even when these have seemed most open to constructive change.

As a working guide to understanding what has happened, what happens now, how does this explicatory model, if one may call it that, stand the test of experience? What does it have to tell, for example, about events as violent and disturbing as those of the Nigerian civil war?

Nigeria is a good case to look at, because this large and various country is in important ways a microcosm of the continental situation, and reflects, in one degree or other, all the factors that are now in play.

Carved as "an arbitrary block" out of West Africa — the description is Dame Margery Perham's — Nigeria was administered during its first half century as two countries rather than one. Its northern two-thirds were amalgamated with its southern third in 1914, and this formal amalgamation was confirmed by the Clifford constitution of 1922. At the same time, however, the 1922 constitution excluded the northern region from the first cautious steps towards some form of representative rule.

This meant that the northern two-thirds remained, until 1946, in more or less complete isolation from the trends and currents of nascent nationalism and modernizing thought that began to flow in the south, during the 1930s or even 1920s, as well as from any least participation in electoral exercises.

The thirty-eight emirate authorities of the north were retained as the instruments of "indirect rule": rather like the hereditary authorities of British India, this northern region constituted a "Nigeria of the princes." As such, these emirates were allowed and even encouraged to evolve forms of autocracy that were almost certainly more arbitrary than any they had known in precolonial times.[17] Here again — as in some other well-known cases, whether in French or British Africa — colonial policy buttressed the positions of traditionalist rulers whose approach to any form of anticolonial emancipation became, accordingly, still more reluctant or downright hostile.

Meanwhile, in the south, the politics of reformist nationalism grew vigorous with the rising pressures of European-educated groups and individuals who sought, often skillfully, often courageously, to bend the language of the "civilizing mission" to the advantage of anticolonial emancipation. Using all the experience of their own political tradition, these men spoke with the confidence of those who had well mastered the necessary idiom. Their duty, as they understandably saw it, was to shape the future; just as understandably, they reasoned that there was no one else who could do this.

"It must be realized, now and for all time," wrote the Yoruba leader, Obafemi Awolowo, as early as 1946, "that this articulate minority are destined to rule the country. It is their heritage. It is they who must be trained in the art of government, so as to enable them to take over the complete control of the affairs of their country."[18] Like others of his kind, Awolowo saw this élite as the natural inheritor of British power; and the British, once they had come to reconcile themselves to the idea of political withdrawal, were soon brought to regard things in the same light. But if that was true of the south, it was anything but true of the north. And this was where an inflamed regionalism, becoming "tribal nationalism," began most sorely to make itself felt.

When populist nationalism emerged powerfully on the scene during and after the Second World War — with the growth of the Europe-educated groups, with the return of soldiers from foreign battlefields, with the expansion of primary schooling — it was steered, and steered itself, into a compromise between the demand for Nigerian independence on one hand, and, on the other, the reservations of the British as well as the reservations of traditional authorities whose base was ethnic and was therefore *regional*. So it came about that advance towards independence in Nigeria went hand in hand with the deepening of regional divisions.

The Richards constitution of 1946 gave the north some representation in a central legislative council under colonial control. But it also introduced three regional councils: one for the predominantly Hausa-Fulani north, one for the predominantly Yoruba west, and one for the predominantly Ibo east. These regions, too, had been "arbitrary blocks" carved out of Africa, but once established, like Nigeria itself, they had come rapidly to have a life of their own.

The MacPherson constitution of 1951 carried the process further. It recognized Nigerian unity, of course, but it transformed the regional councils into regional legislatures with regional executives, still of an advisory nature but, increasingly, as the presumptive political heirs of the future.

Now it was that the old counterposing of north and south began to take its full effect. With the traditional leaders of the north very fearful by this time that they were going to be outmaneuvered and in some way subjected to the new politicians of the south, the 1951 constitution soon broke down. Two years later the then British Colonial Secretary, Oliver Lyttelton (the late Lord Chandos), "regretfully decided that the Nigerian

Constitution would have to be redrawn to provide for greater regional autonomy."[19] This was duly provided in yet another constitution, introduced in 1954. Under strong southern pressure there then followed the granting of regional self-rule to the two southern regions, while the vast northern region, reluctantly and suspiciously, moved into a hesitant acceptance of the same autonomy in 1959. And one year after that Nigeria became independent as a federation of three regions governed by groups whose major loyalty, in each case, was far less to federal unity than to regional separatism.

One may argue, of course, that nothing else was feasible; one may also argue the desirability of devolution. The fact remains that after 1953, if not earlier, the whole drive and emphasis of nationalism lay in the separate and competitive advancement of three regional constellations of rival power; and it was above all from this and from its circumstances that trouble flowed. The three major political parties were supposedly federal; in fact, they were nothing of the kind. One of them had a little support outside its own region but the other two had none at all, while the party in the north was far less a political party than a coalition of hierarchical rulers.

Once again, one notes the contradictory nature of colonial policy. The British were in favor of a united Nigeria for reasons of their own: so much was made repeatedly clear. On the other hand, their buttressing of traditional rulers in the north, and their promotion of élites who could be expected to tread a safely orthodox path in the south, produced, and could only produce, powerfully centrifugal forces, and these could be held in check only by an artificial emphasis on centralism.[20]

Thus launched, Nigeria was soon in uproar. With the balance of power in the regions, the central legislature consisted of men who were little more than deputies for their respective regional parties. None of the senior leaders of these parties sat in that legislature: whatever might happen there was in large part a function of regional calculation, not of federal interest. More than that, the northern rulers secured a built-in dominance of the central legislature by virtue of the north's weight of voters. It was another recipe for trouble.

As before 1960, the northern leaders stood pat upon their positions, opposing all serious reform towards the elective principle in their vast region, actively suppressing the democratic radicals who now emerged in Kano and one or two other northern towns, dragging their feet in the field of educational and other social change.

The gap between themselves and the southern leaders rapidly widened as the latter used independence to expand the educational system and the exercise of parliamentary politics. Yet this widening gap soon went together in the two southern regions, now joined by another southern region in the midwest, with an increasingly bitter rivalry for local advantage, and, individually, for the advancement of personal careers which could ensure wealth and power along the lines of the "middle-class solution."

Almost on the morrow of independence, and even before it, these men were blamed for their lack of devotion to the public cause. "There are not many leaders in Nigeria today," a Nigerian writer was complaining as early as 1960, "with the vision to look beyond their immediate personal or sectional interests."[21] Still harsher words had gone before this. For the late Adegoke Adelabu, a dissident Yoruba nationalist writing in the 1950s, the new "middle class" were a bunch of "pot-bellied plutocrats" whose "new hats, gaudy ties, fashionable suits, shining limousines . . . and all the gaudy paraphernalia of the *'nouveau riche'*" were "a pleasure to small children, an entertainment to young girls, the envy of the Junior [Civil] Service, an embarrassment to their soberer supporters, an eyesore to the intelligent public, the laughing stock of veteran nationalists," but also, prophetically, "just the keg of gunpowder needed to set fire to the discontent of the oppressed masses of Nigeria."[22]

Such complaints might be understandable. But they were unrealistic. The men of this nascent "middle class" were merely acting out their neocolonial role, and within a framework which supposed that the national interest, the creation of a bourgeoisie capable of building a capitalist system, was best promoted by serving one's personal interest. Those who called for a different framework, for some kind of noncapitalist framework, had long been excluded from public life, and would so remain. The colonial situation, and thus the heritage derived from it, had no place for them.

Disaster arrived by a devious course. The regions governed themselves increasingly as though they were separate states, and yet were held together by economic ties which could not easily be cut; nor were there many who really thought they should be cut. All the same, the rivalries deepened. They came to be centered, at one crucial point, in the capital of Lagos. Administratively, Lagos lay in the western region. But the western region was now in permanent opposition inside the federal legislature to a coalition of the other two parties. Not too surprisingly, breakdown began in the west.

In 1962, the Action Group Leader of the western region, Awolowo, was found guilty of political offenses by a federal high court and sent to prison.[23] A minority government under S. L. Akintola was then installed by strong-arm methods imposed by the federal government: in practice, by a government under northern control.

This minority government was strongly resented in the west, not so much out of any great love for Awolowo but for its origins in northern support, for reasons of intraregional resentment, and perhaps above all for the personal corruption and self-enrichment which it was widely believed to stand for. When Akintola sought to buttress his authority by regional elections in October 1965, he could win them only by rigging and repression. "Key election officers were kidnapped," reported *Time* magazine, "key opposition candidates kept off the ballots entirely."

There followed, at once, something like a rural uprising. Dozens and perhaps hundreds of people were killed in outbursts of protest in the western region. And it is in this uprising that one finds the true key to most of what followed later. For it was a protest, above all, against what I have termed "the middle-class solution": against the whole basis, that is, upon which the inherited problem had predicated its own resolution. An eye-witness described the uprising, in my view rightly, as "a revolt of the peasants against the ruling politico-business clique and its kulak-type local adherents, who in practice bore the brunt of the popular anger. Cars, cocoa plantations, and 'better' houses were destroyed with the great-

66

est zest."[24] Elsewhere, too, the currents of this popular anger against ministers and functionaries who were notorious for their "primitive accumulation," by foul means or fair, now grew into a storming tide of disaffection. The hopes that men had cherished of a better life began to seem distant, and independence a mockery of broken promises.

In January 1966 a handful of young officers, mostly Ibo, conspired to kill several prominent leaders of the major parties, and largely succeeded. Their program, insofar as they had any, aimed at clearing the country of corruption and building a new unity.[25] They were swept aside almost at once. Power was assumed by General Aguiyi-Ironsi, who had little idea of what to do with it. But riding the waves of southern popular support for the January coup, he abolished the federal structure; declared Nigeria a unity of thirty-five provinces with purely local powers; and, still sharper provocation of the north, enacted the complete federalization of the regional civil services. Northern groups interpreted all this, whether sincerely or not, as an Ibo plot to dominate the north, and while contemplating their own possible secession from Nigeria, struck back without mercy, killing Ironsi in June, and setting up their own military regime at the center. Events now swept along with terrifying force. The Kano communal riots of the 1950s were repeated on a massive scale. Thousands of northern Ibos were slain, thousands more expelled. Nigeria was already at war with itself.

The first federation died, and there were few to mourn it. Yet the federal idea survived. Not only did the north not secede, but its new spokesman, a northern officer,

Yakubu Gowon, tried somehow to hold things together. As the Ibo east withdrew increasingly within itself, a plan evolved for a new federation, eventually announced in May 1967 as part of the maneuvering of that frantic time. The country would be divided into twelve regions: three in the east and three in the midwest and west, but also six in the north. With this grouping, if it could be carried through, there should come an end to the northern monolith, and the promise of a new start. The plan was in any case too late. Something else had happened on the day before its promulgation. Rejecting any regionalization of the east, the military governor of the predominantly Ibo area, Colonel Odumegwu Ojukwu, declared for secession, and proclaimed the Republic of Biafra on the whole territory of what had so far been the eastern region. "Tribal nationalism," this time by way of the Ibo bourgeoisie and its supporters in the east, had reached its logical conclusion.

Subsequent events confirmed this. Though starting as an attempt to give the bulk of Ibo people a new security within a state of their own, the secessionist attempt was not long in degenerating into something rather different: into an attempt to provide the rising Ibo "middle-class" with a new sovereignty of its own. Had it succeeded, an independent Biafra must have reproduced within itself the sectional and ethnic conflicts of Nigeria, not only because it would have been ruled by the same kind of men, and with the same kind of motives, as the old eastern region, but also, what was often overlooked abroad, because it would have denied autonomy to about a third of its population, the Delta peoples who wished neither for secession nor for Ibo hegemony.

The end of the war confirmed the nature of its origins. It brought a widespread and undoubtedly popular sense of relief that the old structure was gone and, with it, the old politicians. This relief was linked to a sense of renewal which often appeared to generate a feeling that here at last, in 1970, was the true beginning of Nigerian independence. That the victors proceeded at once to show a striking magnanimity towards the vanquished was no doubt another factor in this general sentiment of relief and renewal. What was more, the end of the war was followed by vigorous action towards realizing the twelve-state structure promulgated by General Gowon in 1967 on the eve of the war.

All this gave practical force to the hope that the peoples of Nigeria had shaken free of their colonial heritage, and could now begin to build a new and viable system of their own, whether local or federal. Yet if problems of form were now much eased, problems of content remained little different from before. Twelve or more states might certainly be less difficult to govern from a federal center than four states: the question still remained, how were they to be governed? For the time being they were governed by members of the armed forces in association with politicians untainted by the corruption of the first federation (1960–1967); and the military announced that they would stay in power till 1976. But what then? If military government were not to be a permanent arrangement, some alternative must be found.

If this alternative were to be a variant of the same old "middle-class solution," duly wrapped up once more in parliamentary garments, what guarantee could there be that national parties will not once again degenerate into sectional parties, regional parties, get-rich-quick parties, and do battle with each other once again for local interests at the expense of the general interest? If the first federation had come to grief in operating a process of class stratification for the benefit of "pot-bellied plutocrats," as Adelabu called them, rudely but in words that carried a certain ring of truth, why should the second federation end any differently: unless, of course, it could begin to operate a quite different process, a process of egalitarian democracy altogether foreign to the needs and ethos of an evolving capitalism? But what chance could there be of this with the great oil bonanza of the 1970s getting into its stride, and with the central government determined to carry through policies aimed at building private enterprise in industry and commerce, and indeed in every other field of the economy?

So far, in short, the question of socioeconomic system has been answered as before. Perhaps there can be no other answer, or serious consideration of another answer, for a long time to come. Theoretically, at least, a semi-permanent military government can act as the shield of a nascent bourgeoisie until, in the years ahead, this bourgeoisie grows strong enough to impose its political and cultural as well as economic hegemony, and so introduce, at last, a parliamentary democracy on the Western model. If so, the problem of socioeconomic system will be resolved, at least for the foreseeable future. If not, the question of another answer will then become a practical one, and Nigeria may expect to pass into a phase of radical struggles for a new society.

Prophecies would be foolish. What can be asserted

on the evidence to date is that the prospects of the present "middle-class solutions' " being able to achieve general stability and progress, steadily transforming Nigeria into what is called a "developed" country, do not seem good. They are no doubt better in Nigeria than anywhere else in black Africa, for Nigeria is a big country with a relatively large population and with great material resources. But so was the China of the Kuomintang, and yet Chinese capitalism entirely failed in its national mission. And if that comparison be thought unfair, one may perhaps reply that so is Brazil; and yet Brazil, after many decades of trying to build a bourgeoisie capable of creating and operating a parliamentary capitalist system, is still in the throes of "underdevelopment with military rule of a most un-Nigerian harshness," and shows small sign, as things stand now, of emerging from them.

Or again, if non-African comparisons seem out of place, what of the evidence in Africa itself? In one country after another, so far, the attempt to achieve an all-round national development by means of this "middle-class solution," a solution of "private enterprise" buttressed by state enterprise, has written a record of bitter failure. That is the evidence of Nigeria under the first federation, and the evidence of Ghana too. The story is not at its end, and there are other claimants such as Ivory Coast upon the scene. All the same, the weight of this experience until now points toward failure. But if this is the conclusion that speaks from the political record, that of the economic record appears to state it with an added strength.

CHAPTER THREE

The Force of Economics

Nigeria became independent in 1960. So, too, did a scatter of small or very small colonies of the French African Empire, such as Dahomey and Togo, as well as several large but thinly populated ones, such as Chad and Mali. Thus the decade began with a well-marked salute to the ideas and drives of African emancipation. Independence and its opportunities were there; it remained only to realize them. How should this be done?

In that same year, as it happened, there was also launched upon the world a book which claimed to have the answer. This book was the work of a well-known American economic historian, professor at the Massachusetts Institute of Technology and for some time a special adviser to the U. S. President, whose name is Walt W. Rostow. His book's title is *The Stages of Economic Growth.*

It is a book that has been widely attacked by other economists, and today, perhaps, there may be few who take it seriously. Yet this book of Rostow's, in a large sense not always acknowledged, undoubtedly became the customary guide among the orthodox as to what could and should now happen in the whole great field of Africa's development towards societies of much higher production and consumption. Not only had it been re-printed sixteen times by 1968, becoming a cherished text for "development courses"; more than that, it enshrined in print the general run of ideas that were current, in those years, among a whole range of more or less vehe-ment people: experts and advisers in newly independent countries, teachers of economics in newly established business schools endowed by United States or other foundations, makers of policy and assorted political prophets, whether inside Africa or not. It ideologized, often brilliantly, what was otherwise a habit of thought, a nexus of assumptions, a general approach. It defined where the ex-colonies ought to be going, and how they ought to get there.

Its chief argument is familiar, but I will briefly sum-marize it. Rostow says that all societies, no matter how diverse in their origins and history, can be identified "in their economic dimensions, as lying within one of five categories; the traditional society, the preconditions for take-off, the take-off itself" — described as "the interval when the old blocks and resistances to steady growth are finally overcome" — then, fourthly, "the drive to matur-ity, and [lastly] the age of high mass-consumption."[1]

Publishing his book as what he called a "non-com-munist manifesto" — which he appears, with rather more than a touch of Texan panache, to have thought of com-parable significance with that other manifesto of 1848 — Rostow went on to identify the consummation of "take-off," the soaring of the undeveloped into the skies of wealth and comfort, as being necessarily *capitalist* in nature, and broadly comparable with the condition of the United States after the Second World War. He preached the absolute and crucial need for "a new élite, a new leadership," as he put it, which could be only of a capitalist nature, duly licensed by what he termed "an appropriate value system."[2] If that were assured, the rest would follow: just as, he argued, it had always followed elsewhere. As you see, he provided the "middle-class solution," the capitalist road to development, with a respectable integument of theory.

There were critics, true enough, who had little trouble in demolishing this model. Yet the model was widely followed; and it is still worthwhile considering its defects.

To begin with, the bundling of all societies into the same crudely linear concept of developmental process ignored the bulk of human history. To argue that Africans were undeveloped or underdeveloped peoples was tantamount to saying that they had *no history* of their own: whereas, in fact, it lies beyond any serious question that they were in no way undeveloped or underdeveloped in terms of their own frameworks. On the contrary, they had developed their societies from Stone Age simplicity to Iron Age complexity; they had passed from one stage to another of technological achievement. If these peoples were undeveloped or underdeveloped in 1960, this could only be in terms of the quite different history of quite different peoples.

What was this different history? Rostow, and all those who agreed with him, presented the process of mechanization, industrialization, modernization, as an *evolution-*

ary process from one developmental phase to the next. Yet it was very clear, as was remarked at the time, that his "take-off" was nothing but another term for what had long been known as "industrial revolution."[3] Could it seriously be held that England's "industrial revolution," or Scotland's, or that of any other country, was an evolutionary reshaping of society, rather than the displacement of existing structures and relationships by new and different ones? Did those triumphant bourgeoisies simply grow, like Topsy, till they quietly assumed, and were quietly allowed to assume, the mantle and reality of power in the state? Were all those conflicts and upheavals of seventeenth, eighteenth, and nineteenth-century Europe the mere echoes of gradualist reform?

There were few who thought so at the time, and there are not very many who have thought so since. The great productive "take-offs" of that period were not, in any essential sense, the outcome of a reformist modification of existing structures and relationships, whether economic or political or cultural. Unless historians have got it all wrong, which is possible but unlikely, these "take-offs" were the product not of evolution but of revolution.

The metaphor of the poacher who turns gamekeeper occurs to one again. As portrayed by Rostow and the many who have followed him, this ideology for Third World development was really no different from that of the no-holds-barred tycoon who, after due arrival at the respectability of lands and large estate, now becomes a most law-abiding citizen and insists upon the beauties

75

of established order. The newly enfranchised peoples, or such of them as could read, were asked to regard with awe and admiration the splendid continuities of smooth and peaceful self-adjustment by which, it was explained, the blessed Western Europeans and North Americans had arrived at work, wealth, and happiness.

Having now in their turn regained command of their own history, as it was supposed, the Africans were invited to steer along quietly to the same destination by a mere copying of Europe's *present* structures and value-systems, while taking not the least account of the actual ways by which those structures and values had come into existence. Happy Africans: wasn't the highway broad and clear ahead of them? Let them behave like the tycoon in his sanctified old age, while raising no questions about his rascally youth. And if any rumors of that youth still lingered around the place, retelling them should be deplored as in the worst of taste, or, more disgraceful still, as displaying a nasty proneness for subversion.

And so, in economic terms, the political contradiction in late colonial policy — the contradiction between the needs of democracy and the needs of building a privileged élite — was again offered as a coherent and harmonious solution. The Africans were to build their own capitalist systems, this being their only means of progress. But they were to build these systems without any radical or decisive break from the *existing* structures and relationships set in place, whether nationally or internationally, during the outright colonial years. In other words, they were to prove their fitness to govern themselves by attempting what the history of Europe had already shown to be impossible.

It seems to me that there are two chief stages in the argument here.

The first concerns the nature of the economic mechanisms set in place during the last colonial years, and, for the most part, still in place: the structures, one may say, out of which these putative or potential capitalist systems, indigenous, self-generating, are supposed to evolve by a mere process of growth. Quantity, even in Rostow's most non-Marxist manifesto, is to accumulate into a change of quality; and the new quality is to be a full-blown capitalism.

The second stage concerns the nature of the new élites and leaderships, with their appropriate "value systems," who are to be the inheritors of this proposed future.

If things since 1960 have not *yet* gone quite as expected, we are further told by those who follow Rostow's view of things, it is because of Africa's poverty. Let us dispose of that explanation. In fact, the argument has little to do with Africa's poverty, and the little that it has to do with it is not decisive. This is not only because the countries of much of Africa possess great potential wealth: for example, they hold perhaps a third of the world's prime potential in hydroelectric power, though at present only about a fiftieth of its installed capacity; as well as reserves of valuable minerals by no means yet exhausted, though in some cases moving fairly rapidly towards exhaustion. It is not even because Africa lacks realized capital assets. For example, it has been pointed out that per head of population, the Ghana of twenty years ago had about the same amount of capital as did Japan.[4]

The reason why the argument is not about poverty is because the structures and relationships now in place, whether national or international, do not allow Ghana, or any but a small part of the continent, to utilize the sum of its own actual or potential surplus. Japan has been able to develop, from a capital basis not greatly superior to that of the better endowed African countries, because Japan has been able to exercise a far-reaching sovereignty over its own economy. Ghana fails, as do other countries like Ghana, because a substantial part of its annual surplus has continued to go abroad, whether by the workings of the terms of trade, or by company and individual transfers of one kind or another, or by the need to meet an ever-growing burden of service on debts. All the scenarios for African development such as those elaborated by writers like Rostow, and they are legion, give us "Hamlet" without the prince or at least without his father's ghost. They claim to be showing us the drama as it really is: in fact, they have rewritten it on imaginary terms of their own.

We might begin to see the drama as it really is with a crude example. It may be all the more useful, as a basis for comparisons, because it comes from a bluntly colonial situation.

In July 1971 the *Financial Times* of London, a newspaper well attuned to the kind of ideas presented by Professor Rostow, reviewed the recent history of the Portuguese territory of Angola, in every respect a colony save in name, and informed its readers that the years 1962–1969 could be regarded as Angola's period of "take-off." It seems unlikely that Rostow himself would have gone as far as that;[5] never mind, Rostow's essential notion was not being misapplied, for rapid economic growth, no matter what its circumstances, was being equated with systemic development.

And the growth was impressive. Angola's growth of industrial output — the output, that is, of products salable for cash — rose at an average annual rate of 17 percent during those years of 1962 to 1969. The value of its mineral exports actually doubled between 1965 and 1970, reaching a total of £170 million (about $391 million).

But does this signify development in any meaningful sense? None of the growth, we should note, was the fruit of new relationships and structures. The boom took place within the same structures and relationships as before. It was restricted, that is, to the enlargement of a modern sector, or at least of a modernizing sector, from which the bulk of the population, perhaps 90 percent, was excluded except as cheap labor which might also be forced labor concealed only by a system of national labor contracts. Outside this "contract" system, the bulk of the population continued to live within a traditional and *non-modernizing* sector, just as it had before. Within it, they were the helpless objects of a direct exploitation. "What was being developed, accordingly, was not the country as a whole, supposing this to include its five million Africans as well as its three hundred thousand whites, but the extractive system already in place."[6]

The only substantial difference here was that the principal beneficiaries overseas were joined by others. In 1964, driven by financial stringency, the Lisbon regime opened its colonies to the relatively unrestricted inflow of foreign capital, and a correspondingly unrestricted outflow of dividends. To the point, indeed, as the *Financial Times* also noted, that "the foreign investor [now] enjoys a higher priority" in dividend-transfer than the Portuguese investor.

And it was this, above all, that enlarged the boom of the 1960s. In 1963 the proportion of foreign private investment was reported as being less than 15 percent of gross capital fixed formation: by 1969, however, this proportion had risen to about 25 percent, and today is almost certainly higher than that. Most of the new investment has gone into mineral extraction: the boom, in practice, has been a mining boom of classical colonial type. Within it, no doubt, there have been some "spin-off" benefits for blacks as well as whites: those for blacks, as in the earlier Northern Rhodesian (Zambian) case, have certainly been minimal. Figures for 1967–1970, for example, claim the creation of fewer than 30,000 new jobs in transforming industries.[7] This may be little more than the demand for such jobs by new white applicants who have emigrated from unemployment in Portugal.

The economy has remained in any case of completely colonial type. If cotton exports rose by about four times between 1967 and 1970, very few bales of Angolan cotton were being processed into textiles in Angola. To see all this as the development of a country, and not as the mere growth of an extractive sector of its economy, owned almost entirely abroad, would be to mistake a sow's ear for a silk purse. It is only another exercise in making money out of colonial exploitation.[8]

It may be argued in further defense of the viability of a "middle-class solution" that the growth of existing structures and relationships, in this case the growth of an extractive system based on maximizing export of primary products, will in itself lead over time to the emergence of a national bourgeoisie, and thus to the emergence of a capitalist class, and thus to a qualitative change of system. There is nothing in colonial experience which will be found to give the least support to that argument. Only the South African experience does that. Yet the industrialization of South Africa has derived from a caste-and-color structure which is itself a sort of supercolonialism; and no rational observer today, I suppose, will care to assert that growth of the white economy in South Africa is equivalent to development of the country as a whole.

In the case of Angola, in colonial terms by no means a particularly extreme case, the evidence will not even support the view that a white-settler or caste-bound bourgeoisie can emerge. In spite of verbal and even constitutional gestures towards territorial autonomy,[9] lately announced in Lisbon, the dominant white minority in Angola remains the mere agent or intermediary of external interests. How true is this was demonstrated during a recent session of the Legislative Council in Luanda: a council, of course, that is legislative only in name. A leading spokesman for settler interests, Venancio Guimaraes, pointed out that they were having to import Portuguese wine, of which Angola consumes some 25 million gallons a year (wine thus being Portugal's most valuable export to the colony), at prices that were nearly *four times* as high as the export price of comparable wines, free on board, from countries such as Spain and Algeria. And this was only one example: the price of imported Portuguese textiles, the second most valuable export to this cotton-producing colony, was another. "You make us buy for ten here," this settler spokesman complained to the governor, "what we could otherwise buy for five; and you make us sell for five what we could otherwise sell for ten."

Nor is the balance of gain any better for the local whites in respect to much of the capital investment "boom." Such of its profits as do not go freely abroad are channeled into the coffers of a local colonial government entirely in the hands of Lisbon, being then used for whatever purpose Lisbon may decide, and mostly for the financing of Lisbon's wars. Thus the Cabinda Gulf Oil Corporation informed the United States Congress at the end of 1970 that it had already paid some thirty million dollars in local taxes.[10] Since then, Gulf must have provided a much larger sum in hard currency, and, with other such investors, has become a valuable and even indispensable source of revenue for Lisbon's military enterprises.

Now it is obvious that many settlers are doing quite well out of such investments. They are not getting the lion's share of locally realized profits, but they are certainly getting the jackal's share, and, as a group dominant within the local structure, they are wealthier than they were a few years earlier. They remain, nonetheless, within a structure totally subjected to an external system, and their prospects of growing into a class capable of creating and operating a settler system of local capitalism, along South African lines, appear so small as to be effectively nonexistent. These privileged whites may well dispose of cheap labor on terms of advantageous as any available to the employers of late eighteenth-century

England or early nineteenth-century France. But they do not have the possibilities for capital accumulation which those Europeans possessed; and you cannot build a capitalist system without accumulating capital. Angola's capital accumulates, but elsewhere.

All the same, it may be urged, Angola is a colonial situation, as Northern Rhodesia was. Once colonies achieve political independence, they become able to use their new sovereignty so as to modify their structures in the measure of their countries' need for an overall growth which can then lead on to systematic development. There is some truth in this. Yet it is easy to overestimate the degree of freedom, within existing relationships, which these new countries enjoy. Most of the evidence, so far, suggests that even this argument will not hold.

Thus there is nothing to show any systematic difference between colonial *mises en valeur,* such as those of Northern Rhodesia or Angola, and the booms of certain ex-colonies during much the same period. Perhaps the only significant difference is that the number of local beneficiaries becomes larger than before. More crumbs fall from the table; more people pick them up.

Liberia, for more than a century, was a colony of black settlers living from the enterprise of large companies, and for much of the period of one large company, Firestone Rubber, which these settlers in no sense controlled. But there was present here, and from early times, that kind of "new élite" postulated by Rostow as the agent of constructive change; and this élite, beyond any doubt, was well endowed with a "values system" conformable to capitalism.

Yet no local capitalist system appeared, or even began

to appear. All that happened was that the élite became the agent of its foreign — in this case, North American — economic regulator. No doubt the last two decades of government presided over by the late President William V. S. Tubman did something to change this. Liberia became more than, and different from, a simple colony of dependent settlers. It acquired coherence as an entity on its own. Yet it will be hard to argue that the basic sociopolitical and economic relationships have changed, or, at least, that change has given rise to a fully fledged capitalist system. In all essentials, Liberia appears to remain within the same external system as before, and, willingly or not, its dominant groups continue to act, in substance, as the local intermediaries of foreign enterprise.

Yet this, be it noted, is not for any lack of growth. Tubman's rule was epitomized by strikingly successful growth. Liberia's economy, during the 1950s alone, may even have expanded at a rate that was higher than that of any other country in the world. Money incomes quadrupled in that time. Government revenues expanded eightfold. All this said much for Liberian enterprise and energy, but it still left open the question of development, as distinct from mere growth.

A team of American experts, appointed by the most orthodox United States Agency for International Development, could still conclude, in 1962, that the overall system had not been changed by all this growth; that Liberia was indeed growing, as they said, but just as certainly was not developing. If money incomes had quadrupled, so had imports. If government revenues had octupled, they had been spent "for the most part," said these experts, "in ways that do not apparently increase the productive capacity of the nation."

So depressed were these good Americans by what they found that they labeled their report with a title that is memorable, because it neatly defines the whole process in play: they called their report *Growth Without Development*. And the essential reason for this absence of development, they explained, was that an "enormous growth in primary commodities produced by foreign concessions for export has been unaccompanied either by structural changes to induce complementary growth, or by institutional changes to diffuse real gains in real income among all sections of the population."[11]

Here, in other words, the parallel with any other colony *or* ex-colony, evolving by a partnership between dominant foreign interests and convenient local élites, both enclosed within international structures and relationships whose foundations were built in the nineteenth century, becomes unusually clear. The élites do not grow into an independent bourgeoisie because they cannot do so. They remain the junior partners of an external system upon which, at all decisive points, they must continue to depend.

Could they cease to depend upon dominant foreign interests, and their underpinning structures and relationships, even if they wished? To this question, too, the answer appears to be negative. There is a historical parallel here which may throw some light on their helplessness. From any broad review of the evidence one may reasonably conclude that these new élites, these intended bourgeoisies, are rather in the position of those older African élites, kings and chiefs and traders, who throve or tried to thrive upon the Atlantic trade of precolonial times.

Those "kings, rich men and prime merchants"[12] also took, as the new élites have taken, the only opportunities of economic growth that were open to them, and went into partnership with foreign interests on the only terms available to them. This partnership chiefly concerned the export of African captives, because the primary interest of the external system of those days, that which prefigured the external system of our own times, was in African slaves for cheap labor in the Americas.

From exporting a few captives — the disposable persons of African society, convicted criminals or war prisoners — the kings and merchants were drawn into exporting many; and to export many captives they had to buy them from others who had seized such captives, or they had to do the seizing themselves. Either way, they became a parasitic agency of foreign interests upon which they had increasingly to depend, and upon which, in the course of time, they were willing to depend. They thus deprived Africa of productive labor to the evident enrichment of Western Europe and North America. Some of them saw the unequal balance of gain. Others saw the loss and suffering that were inseparable from the trade. Not a few tried to stop the trade or withdraw from it. Almost none succeeded, or not for long. Only a change of interest in the external system, beginning with the development in England of cheap English labor in workshops and factories, was to prove sufficiently powerful to lift these countries off the hook.

Those old élites who were able to profit from the

slave trade undoubtedly made their economies grow. But it was growth without any systemic development, because their imports had no developmental potential. If anything, these imports had a regressive impact. They tended to supply such things as textiles which, otherwise and previously, were made at home; or they were mere luxury goods, such as gin and rum; or they were firearms and gunpowder which helped still further to enlarge the trade.

It cannot be said that this absence of African development owed anything to the irresponsibility or incompetence of African entrepreneurs: compared with the nabobs of the English sugar trade, they were anything but profligate or spendthrift. They did the best they could to realize and conserve their profits. One recalls the well-known case of Chief Nana of Brohemie Town on the Benin river, in the southernmost part of what became Nigeria, who was ousted by the British navy in 1894 for refusing to share his trade monopoly with British competitors. When Admiral Bedford finally broke through Nana's stockade, he found no fewer than 99,000 bottles of gin in 830 cases.[13]

But the object of this vast provision of booze was by no means orgiastic. Nana bought gin because gin, in those days, was well recognized as a "growth stock," a hedge against inflation so long as the corks and seals held good. Nana was a saving man, and it was scarcely his fault that the best thing he could find to save was gin. Yet the trading profits of the English sugar barons, however plentifully thrown around in high living, also went steadily into the foundations of the industrial revolution: into, that is, national *development* as well as growth.

This, one may repeat, says nothing about individual competence. In terms of individual competence or initiative, the balance may well be thought to fall on the side of Nana and his fellow traders in the Niger Delta: of men, for example, such as Ja Ja of Opobo, who stubbornly tried to break through the English seagoing monopoly of trade. Then, as now, the question of who gains and who loses may have rather little to do with individual competence, probity, or initiative.

At any rate after 1650, the Atlantic slave trade grew large within a relationship of substantive loss on one side and gain on the other: if still in primitive terms, this was a form of colonial relationship. Perhaps one may term it a "paleo-colonial" relationship: most of the African partners in that long period before European invasion retained their political independence. Then followed, in a linked sequence, the central colonial period when independence was lost. Now, today, we have a third colonial period — as it is sometimes called, a "neo-colonial" period — in which Africans once again enjoy their political independence, but within an overall structure which puts narrow limits on their possible use of it; which continues to impose a persistent transfer of wealth from Africa to the outside world; and which ensures, if in new terms, a fresh stagnation or even a regression.

These assertions appear to be true, or largely true, even in those cases which have been most praised as exemplary of a *post*colonial growth and relationship. If the economy of Liberia, for example, has been growing without any corresponding development of a new pattern and system of Liberian society, this owes nothing to a lack of local energy or intelligence, but almost everything to the fact that this growth has concerned the expansion of what exists, without leading on, or leading on as yet, to any qualitative change in what exists. Nor is there any evidence, as yet, that the growth of this particular system can ever lead, in itself, to a qualitative change in the societies here in question.

Turn from Liberia to a country without any such history of settler rule, the neighboring Ivory Coast, independent since 1960. Here, it is claimed, new élites of middle-class type, of bourgeois formation, really are building an independent structure which is on its way towards self-generating capitalism: in other words, towards the displacement of an existing structure by a new and different one. Now the Ivory Coast, during the 1960s, experienced a boom that was comparable in magnitude with that of Liberia a little earlier. This boom began, indicatively enough, *before* the coming of independence: it was not, that is, a product of independence. Between about 1950 and 1965, the Ivory Coast's rate of economic growth is said to have run at an annual average of 9 percent, with rather less at the beginning of the period and rather more, as the boom *accelerated* after independence, towards the end of it. Once again, this was primarily an exports boom: exports quadrupled — not, as in Liberia, of minerals, but of farming products. Coffee exports quintupled; cocoa exports more than doubled; others also rose. They are still rising.

And at first sight the visitor to Ivory Coast may well think that he is seeing the birth of a system which, while modeled on that of France, is becoming independent of France: self-generating, autonomous, increasingly in command of its own destiny. Its capital city of Abidjan erupts with sky-climbing offices and apartment buildings; its luxury shops are indeed full of luxuries, its streets encumbered with private cars. Behind these signs of consumers' prosperity, moreover, there are other indicators of a capitalist-type expansion.

Ivory Coast's urbanized population rose in number from some 160,000 people in 1950 to 650,000 in 1965 — more than times four — and is larger still today. Labor in its booming plantation economy has been increasingly provided by the afflux of unemployed or underemployed rural people from neighboring "pools of stagnation": migrant workers into Ivory Coast from Volta increased over the fifteen-year period from about 100,000 to nearly one million, or almost to a quarter of the whole Ivory Coast population.

Perhaps more convincingly, there is evidence for a shift to money economy. Production of the main items of food consumption increased, it is true, by nearly double in the fifteen years; but this, as rising food imports show, was not nearly enough to feed the new urban dwellers; and it could not be enough because of the heavy emphasis on export-crop production. Food imports, mainly of wheat and rice, rose from 27,000 tons in 1950 to 92,000 in 1965, the latter providing food not only for about three-quarters of all urban consumers, but also for about 14 percent of rural consumers. More and more folk, in other words, have been having to pay cash for their food. Given the mechanisms of the market, this means a steady transfer of wealth from rural consumers to urban traders, and this, of course, is another way in which one would expect a greater class stratification to appear, and, with that, a bourgeoisie.[14]

Yet what does one find, when turning to look at the structures which result from the boom? Certainly there is some emergence of what may perhaps be called an urban proletariat, though scarcely of an urban working class in any European usage of the term. Is there the emergence of a capitalist-forming class? There are many more African plantation owners than before; some of these have large properties. In the towns there are certainly a number of people, perhaps several thousand individuals by the early 1970s, who enjoy a bourgeois style of life and its "appropriate values system," whether as politicians, civil servants, or businessmen associated with foreign enterprises. But it scarcely appears that these élites form even the outlines of a class capable of moving towards, much less exercising, a domestic capitalist hegemony in Ivory Coast.

There has probably been an extension of capitalism in the country. But, remarks Samir Amin, "there is no ground for saying that [this] is the development of an Ivory Coast capitalism. This society" — of "middle-class" pretensions — "has no autonomy of its own; it has no being without the European society which dominates it. Here, the workers are African. But the true bourgeoisie is absent, domiciled in Europe, which provides the capital and the men who use it."[15]

On one side, the greater part of salaries paid at high levels go to Europeans. On the other, export of wealth by transfer of savings, dividends, and other means has meant, we are told, that the whole capital surplus annually generated in Ivory Coast has been finding, and continues to find, its way abroad. Once again, this is undoubted growth, but it is growth without development:

and growth, principally, for the benefit of already established capitalist systems, mainly that of France.

Can it be otherwise? Within present structures and relationships, evidently not. Other examples return the same conclusion. If peanut exports provided Senegal, for example, with an early economic growth, the principal local beneficiaries were and have remained the Mouride brotherhood of planters and operators. Some of these men have accumulated fortunes. Often they have done it by the most classical methods of budding capitalism: by enforcing low wages and ensuring bad working conditions. Yet nobody can suppose that the Mouride network of entrepreneurs represents, in consequence, a nascent capitalist class: rather than that, according to the evidence, it represents another repetition, if under singularly different conditions, of the paleo-colonial contract in the Atlantic slave trade and its overall effects for the African peoples involved.

And we are concerned here, one should recall, with the potentials for major structural change contained within a necessarily long historical process. Capitalist classes are made, not born; and their making requires a number of indispensable conditions. One of these is clear evidence that a superior rate of profit may be had from investment in manufacture, rather than in trade or in the purchase of land and houses. Another is the capacity to dominate, or sufficiently control, the market or markets at home or abroad for which the manufactures are made. All this requires a subtle but severely real exercise of financial and commercial sovereignty by groups whose social status and attachment have become sharply detached from the traditional milieu out of which their capitalism has developed. One needs only to recall the crucial role played by fully urbanized merchant groups in Europe, even by groups whose ethnic, or supposed ethnic, status and attachment were outside, or thought to be outside, the loyalties of established society; in the English case, among others, that of the Jews and the Puritans. It was not the landed aristocracy of eighteenth-century England that founded the English capitalist system, nor was it the civil service, much less the head-masters of elementary schools or the dons of Oxbridge.

None of the commercial or entrepreneurial groupings of independent Africa appears to be in a position to ful-fill these indispensable conditions. Much is made of the "unwillingness" of African businessmen to invest in manufacture rather than in real estate. They are some-times said to be too narrow-minded, too conservative, too much attached to the bird in the hand rather than the covey in the stock exchange. The observation has its truth. Even in Nigeria, which one would expect to be the great exception because of its size and wealth, the prob-lems of evolving an indigenous capitalism appear essen-tially the same as elsewhere.

True enough, Nigeria has a stock exchange with per-haps as many as ten thousand persons or entities holding shares in local companies. True also, the present Nigerian government is doing its best to expand this share-holding enterprise, and set up in April 1973 a bank specifically designed "to aid local businessmen and institutions in buying from aliens small and medium-size businesses," endowing this bank with an initial capital of fifty mil-lion naira (about £31 million sterling).[16] All this again speaks for local intelligence and drive. Perhaps it may be possible to induce an atmosphere in which Nigerian businessmen will regularly prefer buying company shares rather than houses for rent or land for investment. Yet the fact remains that Nigeria, in attempting this enterprise in local capitalism, will still remain enclosed within an external system which, by the nature of economic reality, must continue to dominate it. As in Ivory Coast, the "real bourgeoisie" will still be in foreign lands.

One should not be dogmatic. Nigeria may succeed in this enterprise, partially at least, where others fail: if so, Nigeria will be the exception which proves the rule, and large oil finds may now greatly help it to become so. Yet most such nascent bourgeoisies seem likely to remain, as a shrewd observer lately noted of well-off Ghanaians, "*rentiers* at heart."[17]

But if they are *rentiers* at heart, rather than bold capitalist entrepreneurs, this again owes nothing to any lack of competence or initiative. The point is important if only because one often hears this argument: that African capitalism could flourish if only Africans would "seize their opportunities." And it is true that surplus trading profits, in Ghana or elsewhere, do go generally into houses or cocoa farms or a bigger trading network. Yet who in their circumstances would choose differently? I was reading the other day about the Archduke Franz Ferdinand, heir to the Habsburg imperial throne before 1914. He had inherited, or otherwise acquired, a huge amount of property in land and houses. Did he therefore go into manufacturing and help to enlarge the growth of Austro-Hungarian capitalism? Not he: the bulk of his fortune he kept in land and houses, though he had the

94

best possible banking advisers. And why? Because he was embedded in a family and cultural structure which put the emphasis on landed estate, on direct personal control of one's wealth, on maximal security of investment. It is no different with the Ghanaian businessmen. "The whole social structure and ethos" of their society has reinforced a tendency to keep businesses to within the size which one man [can] manage and, what [is] at least as important, to cream off profits into areas where they [can]not be lost."[18]

And who, things being as they are, will care to say that these businessmen are ill advised? Let them embark on manufacturing, and they are at once confronted with the direct competition of foreign interests far stronger than themselves. They are forced to wrestle with powers which they feel, not without good reason, to be far beyond their range and reach. Even when they channel off a part of their cash surplus into share investment they will do it, if they can, by investment in Europe or North America rather than at home. In this respect, needless to say, they only follow the example of investors in Europe and North America.

The point is a larger one, we see, than security and habit. The operation of the overall system works in such a way that the non-African interest is always on top; that is why growth of what exists seems so very unlikely to accumulate to the point of a qualitative change of system.[19] Here, too, there are suggestive parallels from the past. The lessons are not new. Those old élites of the Atlantic slave trade, once they were obliged to give up slaving and go into new forms of enterprise, such as the plantation production of palm oil for European soap, also tried to challenge the monopolist superiority of foreign interests. One thinks again of Ja Ja of Opobo in the Niger Delta.

This highly instructive case is long forgotten outside Nigeria, but deserves to be remembered. Born in 1821, Ja Ja was outstanding among those self-made men of the Delta who owed their rise to wealth and political power to gifts of intelligence and energy. By the 1860s Ja Ja had become a very successful palm-oil producer and an influential figure in local politics; later, going from strength to strength, he founded a trading state of his own, that of Opobo. A modernizing initiator, his aim was to transform the palm-oil trade of the Delta into a system capable of standing on its own feet. He wanted, that is, to outdo the British traders at their own game.

He soon fell foul of them through opposing their penetration into his markets. The traders duly called on the local British consul, and the consul called on the British navy. This was a setback for Ja Ja but he overcame it. Having done that, he proceeded to try to turn the tables on his European trading partners who were also his competitors, and began penetrating into their markets overseas. He set about trying to get round the British shipping monopoly by chartering vessels that would carry his oil to Europe and sell it directly on the market there, thus benefiting from the same prices as those which British importers could command in Europe. What could have been more laudable from the theoretical standpoint of Britain's "civilizing mission"? Here was a black man who was trying hard to "catch up" with the times, and was doing it with marked success.

But the British were not inclined to praise Ja Ja. On

the contrary, they found him an intolerable nuisance, and even, as a Nigerian historian has observed, "the greatest impediment to their occupation of eastern Nigeria."[20] They moved in on him with force and simply removed him from the scene. Officially he was "deported" for "treaty breaking"; in fact, his "deportation" was a calculated act of economic warfare. And what they did with Ja Ja, they then applied to others of the same kind and ambition. "With Ja Ja's 'deportation', the process had begun whereby Britain removed all rulers who valued, and stood up for, their independence. Thirteen years after, all the states of the eastern Delta had passed under British rule."[21] The drive for political control on the mainland was powered by the bid for economic control; essentially, it was to be the same everywhere else in colonized Africa.

In our own times the drive for political control has withered from lack of value to the controllers, but it would be merely naive to think that the controllers' interest in economic control, however indirectly or "invisibly" exercised, has done the same. Of course the new élites of the neocolonial contract are not threatened by "deportation" if they fail to toe the line, though they may be threatened by other measures of political coercion which have the same effect. But they are certainly just as much threatened, if they embark on "adventures," by the bankruptcy court. Or that at least is what they believe; and if they believe it there must be reasons for their belief.

These reasons are not hard to trace. We have touched on some of them already. What the overall system demands — the system in which these African businessmen are enclosed — is the export of African primary products in return, substantially, for the import of manufactured goods. Little in this respect has changed since outright colonial times. If foreign interests support the building of an aluminum smelter in Ghana, this is not in order to process any of the 200 million tons of bauxite ore estimated to be available for mining in that country. On the contrary, none of this Ghanian ore is scheduled for exploitation. What the smelter smelts is West Indian or other African ore.[22] If foreign interests support the mining of bauxite in Guinea, they do not support the smelting of it there. They smelt it in other countries. In such ways as this the old pattern of dependence is extended by new methods: the country with ore extraction has no smelter, and the country with the smelter has no ore extraction. What African businessman can hope to be able to make a dent in that pattern?

Such examples are many. The little country of Gabon, one of the old colonies of French Equatorial Africa, has huge iron ore deposits; much manganese ore, among the largest deposits in the world; useful quantities of uranium ore. Its population in 1970 was around the half-million mark. It was also thought to be among the more deprived of African populations, having gained relatively little even from such colonial benefits as preventive medicine: here, at least, the rate of population growth appears to have remained a small one. Clearly, Gabon's vocation, from any rational viewpoint, should be to develop and prosper as a major source of industrial wealth for a whole cluster of African populations.

But what has happened? Once again, we have a boom in mineral exports to Europe and North America, a growth without any structural change, without any true development: and, incidentally, with absolutely no benefit to Gabon's neighboring populations. The iron ore goes largely to Bethlehem Steel in the United States; the uranium enables France to make nuclear weapons. The essential contract is exactly the same as it used to be in outright colonial times. Another tiny country, Togo, with about two million people, enjoyed an initial *mise en valeur* — if "enjoyed" is the right word — long ago under German colonial rule. Today it enjoys another, this time through the export of its huge deposits of phosphate for fertilizers, none of which is processed in Togo. Nor do the big countries escape similar consequences of this kind of "development."

If the new élites proposed by Rostow and those who follow him as the pioneers of an African capitalism, heading for "take-off" on American lines, still refuse to become capitalists, and prefer the safety of their subsidiary or salaried role in the export booms of today, they are not, as can be seen, turning their back on "opportunities." All such perspectives as those defined by the prophets of a capitalist solution, in the sense that we have been talking about, fail to be realized because the essential conditions for them are absent. What is actually happening is not the emergence of an indigenous capitalism, but only the extension of the capitalist systems of the outside world.

And here the parallels with Latin America become very evident. We can do no more than glance at them now. Yet it is obvious that the caste and class inheritors of the Spanish and Portuguese empires, in America, were in a far stronger position for the building of indigenous capitalist systems than the new élites of Africa today. But the systems they have built, though certainly in many respects of a capitalist nature, have remained manifestly weak and even regressive: nowhere strong enough, after more than a century if now with one or two exceptions, to defend their peoples from the continued processes of wealth transfer to foreign investors.[23]

What chance, one may ask, have far weaker and less stratified élites in Africa today of achieving the success that has so largely eluded these Latin American élites? Of achieving this, moreover, in a period when the processes of wealth transfer are not getting smaller, but are getting larger, more diversified, more "up to date," more subtle, more exacting? Do I exaggerate here? Scarcely. Africa's payments on debt service, to take only that aspect of the matter, are much greater than they used to be, and are growing fast. In 1966 they were estimated at about 26 percent of gross inflow; the projection is that by 1975 they will have risen to 53 percent. What effort at private or even public accumulation can prevail against so adverse a tide of transfer?

After Ghana's return to parliamentary rule, some years ago, great efforts were made to prevail against that adverse tide. The most orthodox of procapitalist policies were introduced. Yet the results were to plunge Ghana still more deeply into foreign debt, and end in a monstrous currency devaluation. The Ghana High Commissioner in London, addressing the Royal African Society in 1971, was among those who begged for relief. He argued that Ghana had fully embraced the British parliamentary system, and was now "a bulwark against communism." The leader of the opposition was paid two-thirds of the prime minister's salary, and was even "provided with a car and chauffeur."[24] What better proof of orthodoxy could there be? Yet this properly orthodox Ghana would nonetheless require, he said, a total relief from debt payments for a period of ten years if its economy were to recover and move ahead. They were words lost on the wind.

Indeed, a strange situation. The Africans have been asked to act as loyal partners in an overall system which, consciously or not, directly or indirectly, deprives them of any opportunity for true development: of any opportunity, that is, for systematic change from one set of structures and relationships to another and more effective one, whether capitalist or not.

They have been lectured, but endlessly, on the absolute need to eschew "experiments," to refrain from "adventures," to accept obediently the patterns of behavior of their senior partners overseas.

Whenever and wherever they have seriously dissented, tried to act differently, they have been set upon at once, through every conceivable medium of publicity and pressure, and held up to ridicule: as Nkrumah was, as Sékou Touré has been, as Julius Nyerere or Kenneth Kaunda still are. Not only that: their "adventures" find the purse strings of foreign aid drawn strangely tight against them — as again in 1971, for example, when Britain obstructed aid to Tanzania because Tanzania had nationalized assets belonging to British subjects: even to those British Asian subjects whom Britain prefers should stay abroad. Or else inconvenient Africans discover, thanks to some curious working of the world market for primary products, that the prices of their most valuable exports suffer a collapse. And even when they accept defeat and return submissively to the fold of the orthodox, they are likely to find, as the leaders of Ghana have lately found, that their creditors still want their cash.

They are also exhorted to patience. Let them continue as they are and one fine day, it is said, all will be added to them. They too will then soar into the heavens of the blessed, and "take off" into comfort. Yet even in the crude terms of raw-material availability, the doctrine of salvation by growth-of-what-exists must appear at best a dubious one. For if one accepts this doctrine — that Africans can save themselves by the mere growth of their existing economies, though all the evidence, as I have tried to show, suggests the contrary — then it would still require at least several decades for any of these countries to arrive at self-generating industrial development. But can Africans afford to wait?

"To a greater or lesser degree," Professor S. R. Eyre has lately told us in a survey of raw-material resources up and down the world, "one can speak of the imminent exhaustion of the reserves of a large number of essential metals." And the time scale with which this crisis is concerned, he adds, "is to be measured in decades rather than centuries."[25] In the central matter of crude oil — no doubt the foundation for any doctrine of survival by growth-of-what-exists — recent estimates suggest that world resources may reach a 90 percent exhaustion, at the present rate of consumption, "somewhere between the years 2020 and 2030." But it is precisely the period of about half a century, other estimates tell us, that Africa requires in order to achieve prosperity by growth-of-what-exists.

Nuclear energy? Its production in nonbreeder reactors has already, according to Professor Eyre, produced a dire shortage of the necessary uranium. Or again, with thirteen million people in the Netherlands consuming nearly twice as much tin as the whole of Africa; with the United States consuming more than half the world's smelted aluminum, a quarter of the world's copper, more than a third of the world's nickel, and other minerals *pro rata,* with other industrialized countries similarly *pro rata,* how much is likely to be left for an industrially developed Africa, forty or fifty years ahead? Aren't Africans rather likely to be left, at that point, staring at empty holes in the ground?

How can these countries hope to develop an agriculture, corresponding to the structures of the industrialized countries of today, when West Germany alone consumed in 1968 more than twice as much mineral phosphate as India, Pakistan, and Indonesia put together; and when existing deposits of phosphate are, apparently, already of "very limited extent"? What, for example, will West African countries do in the future, when the abundant phosphates of Togo have entirely disappeared, as they quite largely have already, into the soils of Europe? And if these countries cannot develop that kind of agriculture, how will they feed the rapidly growing urban populations which the doctrine of survival-by-growth incessantly demands?

To pose such questions, as you see, is not to make an ideological point, though an ideological point could no doubt be made. Survival by growth-of-what-exists — as presented to us, the case for an evolving capitalism in Africa — appears generally to have little hope, and in most cases no hope at all, of leading on to "take-off," "development," or any other of its proposed objectives. The case for believing this does not rest on preconceived objections of a theoretical sort. It may also rest on such objections: the point here is that it rests on the ascertainable facts of the matter.

Are alternative courses of policy and action possible? Clearly, they must be: that Africa will eventually find the means not only of safe survival, but also of all-round progress, may appear more than possible. What is evidently not possible, meanwhile, is the resolution of Africa's crisis, of the whole network and imbrication of problems which add up to this crisis, by the prolongation or enlargement of existing structures and relationships. That is what the general balance of economic evidence over the past decade and more, like the balance of political evidence, appears now to state with small tolerance for denial. Every "orthodox" effort to escape from growing incoherence, whether within individual countries or between countries, duly wrecks itself upon the rocks of the inherited situation.

Before going on to consider what alternative courses of policy and action Africans have found, or consider they have found, or now believe they must find, it may be useful to look a little further at efforts towards rational reorganization witnessed in these years.

CHAPTER FOUR

Struggles to Escape

Though necessarily rapid, this review has established a central point about Africa's current troubles. These arise from structures and relationships which bar the way to true development, to the change from a colonial system to a postcolonial system, and even, often enough, to a mere growth of what exists.

The recent experience of many countries displays this inherited problem; none more starkly, perhaps, than that of Ghana. It is not simply that cocoa has remained the main support of Ghana's national economy; it is much more that this crop is still produced within the same external structures and relationships as before. Ghana remains, in other words, at the mercy of the world market; and among things merciful on this earth the world market figures a long way down the list.

When Dr. Kofi Busia became prime minister in 1969, the average price of cocoa for that year stood at £422 a ton, having recovered from the catastrophically low price to which it had sunk in the last months of Kwame Nkrumah's regime. But less than two years after Dr.

Busia became prime minister the price went down again, sinking to about £250 a ton. The highly orthodox Dr. Busia, who had already told the world that his spiritual home was the University of Oxford, where they still do carefully today what was useful yesterday or the day before, proceeded to make good the loss by borrowing money from abroad. He borrowed a great deal of money, making Nkrumah's efforts in that direction look singularly modest. By the end of 1971, the Busia government's debt-service obligations had risen by the same steep rhythm with which cocoa earnings had fallen, and to a grand total of about £100 million. With debts thus rising and revenues falling, what conceivable government, no matter how great its obedience and orthodoxy, could hope to make ends meet?

It may be thought that the politicians, bureaucrats, soldiers, and policemen of Africa have much to answer for, especially in terms of obedience and orthodoxy. But very evidently, what they do not have to answer for are the *basic* causes of their countries' troubles.

Such conclusions are not common to us all. Many persons in authority outside Africa, or speaking for authority, have read the evidence in a different way. For them, Africa's troubles come from some inherent inability of black people to cope with their own problems. These authorities have lectured us on the "immaturity" of Africans. They have told us of African tendencies towards moral turpitude and violence; and every time a General Amin has appeared upon the stage, apparently confirming all they say, they have not failed to preach the lesson. Rather as though the recent history of Europe and America were one of sweetness and light, they have harped on the inbuilt irresponsibility which, they say, so regularly causes these black fellows to fail in the arts of self-rule. These peoples, we have been told, were presented with perfectly effective institutions, the best institutions that anyone could have; but they have not been able to work them. They have muddled their start; they have missed their opportunity.

Whether in England or elsewhere, one saw this particular reading of the evidence with an especial clarity during the Nigerian civil war of the late 1960s. All sorts of prominent people then felt it well and wise to voice their disappointment with Nigerians, to whom Britain, as it was said, had so generously conceded responsibility for their own affairs. An English historical writer, Sir Arthur Bryant, is one of those who has put this view of the matter with a touching pathos.

"Of course," he wrote, "we never intended that such disasters [as the civil war] should overwhelm helpless persons to so many of whom our forebears had brought the blessings of Christian and, therefore, libertarian and peaceful civilisation. . . . We never willed the Nigerian tragedy; nothing was further from our minds when, in an orgy of popular self-congratulation" — unshared, we are to gather, by the writer himself — "we divested ourselves of that responsibility [we had held], and bade the Nigerian people to 'go it alone' under the rule of the politicians and administrators we had trained for democratic Parliamentary self-government.

"How could we have expected to anticipate what has happened? Our intentions were generous, noble, and completely blameless: it was only our calculations which were at fault. . . ." Faulty calculations, that is, not as to the validity of those noble institutions which "we" had installed, for the benefit of Nigerians, but as to the capacity of Nigerians to assume and work them. "We" were guiltless: the blame for this sad disaster among the Nigerians must be placed, unless on them, on "the unrealistic idealism of an ill-informed democratic majority in Britain." Left to "ourselves," "we" the élite would obviously have known better. [1]

That may seem a rather complacent statement of a familiar attitude. All the same, it probably expresses what many observers—and, no doubt, many more nonobservers—have thought and still think. One may add that it undoubtedly expresses what many Africans themselves have thought and said about their own leaders. They have watched the venality of men in power, and condemned these men for failing to rise to the occasion. They have deplored the corruptions of public life, and with plenty of provocation for doing so. One recalls, among countless examples, a minister of education who enriched himself by sponsoring schemes to send young men and women for education in Europe, and who sent none, but who still kept the fees he had collected from their families. One remembers a minister of finance whose art of extracting a personal percentage from public contracts passing through his hands became so scandalous as to lead to his assassination by outraged citizens. And to say what the wholesale and reckless waste of public money on ministerial pomp and presidential palaces and first-class airfares and expensive motor cars and all the rest has been like, to no small extent still is like, would be beyond the limits of sober language, not to say diplomatic tact.

Historically, of course, the truth is complex. From that standpoint it can be seen, even now, that *any* attempt to work the institutions taken over from colonial power must have run into more or less acute difficulty, no matter what manner of men had made that attempt. As we have also seen, moreover, much of what has been condemned as venality or corruption was little other, in fact, than a reasonable attempt to accumulate wealth in the hands of a potential bourgeoisie: the very same attempt as that which had characterized English society in the eighteenth century and later. Faced with this challenge to primitive accumulation, Africans can by no means be said to have "missed their opportunity": far from it, they have seized it with an energy and skill which would have been much admired under King George the Third and his successors. The trouble for them is that they have not been living under George the Third, but in a time and place where accumulation, however primitive, cannot take them to hegemony, and so, with hegemony, to an entrenched power and a consequent respectability. There are no longer any prospects, it would seem, for trainee game-keepers.

When one looks at the 1960s from a historical stand-point, seeing that brief period both as outcome and as prelude, the same contradictory picture repeatedly appears. On one hand, there are plenty of reasonable grounds for complaint. The reformist nationalism of the last ten or fifteen years — the attempt to run these countries by a mere reform of the inherited situation — has worked towards strife and frustration. It has led to the concentration of power, and of the benefits that flow from power, in the hands of relatively narrow groups. This, in turn, has led to the persistent breakdown of efforts at international reorganization inside Africa. Internally within these states, it has also led to the growth of a disruptive micronationalism, of the same reformist type, arising far less from any creative desire for cultural autonomy, or for the defense of local interests as a whole, than from rivalries between contending coteries and cliques. And this, again in turn, has undermined representative forms of government to the advantage of military dictatorship. Of all this we know enough, here in Europe and America, to understand that it must sow a harvest of self-doubt and even desperation.

There is much of both on the scene today. Yet the picture also has another side. Here, admittedly, we enter upon ground still more subjective. But the enfolding atmosphere — the way that Africans think and talk and act about themselves and their lives — is not, or so it seems to me, either desperate or self-doubting. The keynote of contention, perhaps, is rather one of bafflement, and of the anger which can ensue from that. Otherwise you will encounter a mental climate that is stubbornly one of confidence, even of optimism. And if you look a little deeper you may find, I think, that this optimism is not the product of a bland or silly insouciance — a Nero's fiddling while the city burns: but, rather, the outcome of a sense of emancipation, of slowly winning through the fogs and mystifications of the colonial period. If men are angry because they are baffled it is also because they believe that solutions *are* possible: these solutions have only to be found.

This kind of confidence in adversity — this most un-European rejection of anxiety — may owe something to the nature of societies well-framed, by history, to relieve the worries of the individual by attaching him or her to a belief in the always immanent virtue of the community. But it also owes something to the actual experience of the last ten or twenty years: to the satisfaction which apparently accrues to any people who, after a long servitude, once more take their fate in their own hands. Or perhaps it is simply that anxiety about the *general* condition of things is an ill peculiar to the rich, and one that the poor can seldom care to afford themselves.

If these peoples have not solved their structural problems, they have at least become free to understand them, and, in the measure of their understanding, to try to solve them. It may be that they have tried to better purpose than the outside world seems often ready to admit.

It can bear repeating here, perhaps, that even the record of the élites is far from purely negative. They were the product of the European colonial system and its overriding concept of the bourgeois nation-state. Inevitably they have worked within that concept. Yet if this European concept seems now to have come near to exhausting its capacity for liberating Africans, imposing as it does an extreme disunity of loyalty and action, it was nonetheless creative of values highly *positive* to these colonized peoples. It could and did afford them a sense of collective identity when they needed it most: of corporate solidarity within familiar frontiers, and of a framework for new forms of cultural self-expression. No one who knew the realities of colonial Africa, or who looks at these realities today in territories still colonial, can doubt that nationalism, even reformist nationalism, has proved a valuable instrument for cultural enlargement and for a widening of the consciousness of personal freedom.

One may well conclude that pseudobourgeois or pseudocapitalist forms of rule can offer no further means of progress. It still remains true that the African independence struggles of twenty years ago, and after, were carried to success by Africa's educated minorities, privileged minorities. All that, too, is in the record. They it was who raised the banners of self-rule and carried them forward, not seldom at a severe cost to themselves in liberty and health; who studied the colonial situation and learned how to make the anticolonial cause prevail; who spoke for the nonliterate millions and found ways, often effective ways, of drawing those millions into their support. They it was, in short, who opened the road to a self-rule which, however imperfect, could alone make possible a conscious and therefore genuine confrontation with problems and situations taken over from the past and the present. As others have said, they gave Africa the opportunity to make its own mistakes, and thus to learn how not to make mistakes.

So it comes about — and we are still on highly subjective ground — that the ideological atmosphere is not for the most part one which suggests stagnation. This experimental period has yielded huge dissatisfactions; but they are not, or not often, the self-eroding discontents of peoples who feel that they have failed. There are certainly some who see matters in much the same light as Sir Arthur Bryant: as being the passage from an established peace and welfare to sudden violence and despair. I doubt if they are many.

For the general African experience has not been of any such transition as that. What these peoples have generally seen and known has been something quite different. The transition, for them, has not been from the gleaming light of European tutelage into the darkness of their own designs. Rather has it been from situations of systematic inferiority, of denied responsibility, of implied or even experienced contempt, into situations where, at least, Africans have recovered or are in course of recovering their self-respect and the right to answer for themselves. The very fluidity and constant political movement of the last two decades — contrasting so sharply with the alienation, the general immobility, the fearful boredom of the politics of foreign rule — have induced a sense of excitement, of an ongoing and dynamic process of almost infinite possibilities, that comes very vividly from the record of these years, and is there today, perhaps, even more than it was before.

This record will be studied for a long time, holding as it does so many keys to what is going to be the history of the next fifty years. Already it illuminates at least two decisive factors in the ideological situation. One of these is the persistent search for clarity about the needs and possibilities of independence, for true bearings on a voyage where the charts have said one thing and actual experiences another. This has meant a passionate if sometimes erratic probing for the truth behind the words and phrases, signals, and directions that have come from the outside world; and, with this, a stubborn if also erratic effort to seize this truth, and make it work to useful purpose. Then the record also shows the second factor we have noticed: alongside native pressures, there is the persistence and subtle advancement of foreign pressures, of interference from abroad. In these years the Africans have had to come to terms with themselves. But they have also had to come to terms with an outside world which had no thought, no matter what it might say to the contrary, of leaving them to find their own way ahead.

To the ideological confusions of the late colonial period and its policies of gradualist reform, there were also added all those, of a different kind, that derived from the consideration of nonreformist or noncapitalist alternatives. If these wore socialist garb, what was this socialism, and how could it apply to Africa? On this, too, advice came in from every side: in one jargon from the West, in another from the East, jangling and conflicting, making little sense or none at all. Driven and further disfigured by the Cold War, ideas were thrown into the arena like the figments of a quite unreal debate, and people were left to grasp them as well as they could, and try to find what they could mean.

The late fifties and early sixties were accordingly a period of intellectual ferment and excitement, and the scene of many strange conclusions. This was the time, for example, when the notion of a specifically "African socialism" first appeared upon the stage, as though the fundamental laws of social development could be, and even were, somehow different in Africa from elsewhere. It was said, quite against the evidence, that Africa had even known its own socialism in the precolonial past, and that this socialism could be revived in new guise. Clever men like Mr. Léopold Sédar Senghor of Senegal or the late Tom Mboya of Kenya took hold of this idea and used it, or tried to use it, as a means of suggesting that the status quo was quite different from what others said it was, and could lead in directions quite different from those in which it was actually moving.[2]

There were others who denounced this as a sleight of hand, and clove to the doctrine as it seemed to come from Marx. But they, too, had their troubles. For the doctrine as it seemed to come from Marx, or as it nearly always came from the Marxists, supposed a set of indispensable conditions which appeared conspicuous by their absence. Where was this working class upon whom, it was pronounced, everything must turn? Where was there anything even resembling a national bourgeoisie? Where lay the debris of feudalism, where the onset of a new capitalism? Men searched and did not find. There was much fervent debate, many a famous battle of the books. Could it be held that African society was already stratified by class? But if not, where lay its means of momentum? And if all history was the history of class struggles, must this be taken to mean that Africa, having no classes that anyone could easily define, had *no* history of its own? For if Marx had really meant all *written* history, it was not what the texts actually said.

Remarkably little illumination became available from outside. When historians of the future look back on these years, they will not fail to be impressed in this context by the helplessness of the Left, outside Africa, perhaps as much as by the deviousness of the Right. The Left, for the most part, had given no thought to the problems of Africa, and assumed, with a curious indifference to probability, that whatever prescriptions might be good for Europe or for Asia, or for America, would also serve for Africa.[3]

This indifference, this ignorance, was reflected in a more practical form by some of the bureaucracies of the communist countries. Offered an unexpected chance of participating in African trade and investment — in Guinea, for example, or in Ghana or in Mali, speaking for the earlier years — they applied their familiar rules as though they were dealing with familiar neighbors; and they committed, in consequence, blunders that were costly from their own national standpoint, for they generally adopted a strong national standpoint, but were even more deplorable for Africans who suffered from such enterprises. That, of course, is another simplification; the results were by no means uniformly negative. Yet it is probably true, as well as relevant, that Africans accepting communist aid had gone through some useful experiences of their own by the 1960s, and understood, more clearly than before, what the needs and possibilities really were. Generally, in this respect as in others, the late 1960s and the present years were and are a time of growing clarity of thought, and even of the rise, here and there, of new and more effective forms of mass organization and of grassroots reorganization.

Another central point, perhaps, is that the ideas of the late fifties and most of the sixties were seldom or never considered as being more than experimental; and sometimes they were window-dressing. In Kenya, for example, no thoughtful person was going to take seriously a national plan for "socialism," whether "African" or not, that was most obviously based on the enlargement and enrichment of an élite along lines which, if ingeniously original at certain points, were generally familiar. When Mr. Oginga Odinga entitled his autobiography *Not Yet Uhuru, (Not Yet Freedom)*, he was not indulging in unrealistic dreams about the scope and possibility of humanity's liberation from past servitudes; he was merely putting into words what almost everyone accepted, even though few might be ready to say so: that the ideas of Kenya's national liberation remained as valid as ever, but were far from being realized.[4]

How to realize these ideas was very much an open question, just as it was very much a new question; and through the now open door came many other notions as little connected with reality as Kenya's socialism or President Senghor's political speculations on the same subject in Senegal.[5] One even began to hear it said, wishfully by some, deploringly by others, that this or that new regime was actually "building socialism," rather as though any one of these countries had acquired, or, in isolation, could possibly acquire, the minimal conditions necessary for any such enterprise. One even heard a President Ahmedon Ahidjo, another claimant to ideological distinction, proclaiming his objective as being "not African socialism, but Camerounian socialism,"[6] surely the oddest application of Stalin's doctrine of "socialism in one country" that the world has so far heard, and in practice, not surprisingly, one that has had nothing to do with socialism but a great deal to do with bureaucratic oppression and arbitrary rule.

Other and far more serious and sincere attempts were made to escape from the inherited situation. There were outstanding leaders and other individuals, in these years, who well perceived the hopelessness of the solutions proposed to them in the name of "free enterprise," and who made dramatic efforts to contrive the beginnings of a viable alternative, whether by state capitalism, bureaucratic centralism, or strenuous exhortation. Each in varying circumstances had to pay a heavy price in isolation and in the severing or reduction of democratic links between leaders and led, voters and ministers, peasants and parties, urban workers and trade union officials. And to make things harder still, each was called upon to face a mounting offensive from the West, piling new problems on those they knew already, while they tried against whatever odds and however unfruitfully to apply the lessons of the East.

The 1960s were thus a period of experimental failure. Yet the experiments were not without value. They helped the Africans towards a closer grasp of reality, to a new freedom of thought and theory, and to the reconsideration of analytical methods and proposals. This has gone to the point where it is probably not too much to say that the ideas that have derived from world revolutionary thought and experience at last began to become "naturalized," during the early 1970s, to the conditions and problems of Africa. If this is true, though obviously in varying degrees of clarity and consciousness, then it will be the results of this difficult process of "naturalization" of radical thought that the years ahead will now unfold and display.

This will happen in diverse ways and in different fields of effort. One of these will be that of intra-African rivalry or cooperation. Here, too, the talk and argument of the past ten or fifteen years can be seen to have had their creative side, for they have gradually led onward to a firmer grasp of reality. Independent Africa is as sorely divided as in 1960. In some respects it is worse divided. Yet the reasons for this division and the disablements that flow from it are clearer now.

The history of the idea of African unity is not a new one. There is an old inheritance here too. For the most part, as one would expect, it is an inheritance of utopian idealism, of the saving visions that men have glimpsed and yearned for in times of hardship or defeat. To it belong the fervent thoughts and writings of American Pan-Africanism, the messianic dreams of African Ethiopianism (of salvation by the doctrines of a specifically African Christianity), of such long-forgotten ventures as the National Congress of British West Africa, even of that grand federal structure of which the leaders of the Rassemblement Démocratique Africain spoke only twenty years ago.

It is in this field of ideas about unity, perhaps better than in any other, that one can see the wide range of problems which have arisen from the imbrication of traditional obstacles to intra-African unity with the persistent play of the colonial inheritance. The case for federal or other organic unity, at least in the field of economics, has often been stated, and seems almost self-evident: where many small units are weak or defenseless, their organization within a common framework or frameworks could give them strength.[7] But the obstacles are evidently formidable.

Not only was precolonial Africa divided into many hundreds of ethnic states or statelike units; there was also the arbitrary colonial carve-up and condensation, together with its nationalist ideology. According to the authorities of the colonial period, it was quite all right for Britain or France to unite previously separate units within a single colony, but sheer rubbish to imagine that a future Africa might and should adopt a different pattern. One sometimes had the impression, in those days, that these authorities imagined that their frontiers possessed an almost sacred life and meaning; and certainly these authorities or most of them did their best to fasten this idea about frontiers upon the élites whom they promoted. After all, in the thought of that time, these frontiers not only gave physical definition to African countries; they also defined European spheres of control or influence or advantage.

The early élites did not see things this way; they saw, much more clearly, the gains that might be had from dismantling the colonial pattern, then still a very new one, and shaping another. All this was ridiculed by the colonial rulers or simply ignored. Their attitude was expressed with a fine literary sarcasm by a British governor of Nigeria, Sir Hugh Clifford, as long ago as 1920. He was countering the efforts of the then active National Congress of British West Africa, a committee of African lawyers and publicists, who, while pressing for separate advance to self-rule in Nigeria, Gold Coast, Sierra Leone, Gambia, nonetheless conceived the future of these colonies as being organically combined. Of such unifying notions, Sir Hugh made short work.

"That there is," he said, "or can be in the visible future, such a thing as a 'West African Nation' is as manifest an absurdity as that there is, or can be, an 'European Nation,' at all events until the arrival of the millenium. . . . The people of West Africa do not belong to one stock and are not of common descent . . . . [They have] no common language . . . no community of religious belief. . . ."[8]

Yet it was this self-same governor, such is the tide of life, who almost at once introduced a single (if still advisory) legislative council for the whole of Nigeria, itself a microcosm of West African diversity, and who called the local British rulers of the Nigerian north to join together, at least symbolizing a putative Nigerian nation, with those of the south. Sir Hugh Clifford might still enjoy his little field-day of sarcastic wit at the expense of the National Congress of British West Africa: historically speaking, it was the National Congress, with its notion of unity in diversity, that was running with the future. The contradictions in the governor's opportunism were sharper even than in theirs.

The contradictions in African thought nonetheless remained. Accepting the concept of the nation-state — and there was nothing else they could do — Africans necessarily raised a major obstacle across the path of interterritorial unification. They were obliged, moreover, to accept this nation-state concept within the embrace of a larger dividing factor: that between the British and the French (or other and lesser) imperial systems. So that independence, when it came, not only brought a riveting of separate and separatist identities, but also a new range of divisive influences. Very few anglophone Africans spoke French on the day of independence, very few francophones spoke English; and this linguistic alienation made it all the harder to confront European policies which sought to conserve spheres of influence or control. Very small and weak for the most part, thirteen of the fifteen nation-states which emerged from the French African empire in West and Equatorial Africa were carried, almost at once, lock, stock, and barrel, into a tight politicoeconomic system centered upon Paris, and guarded in Africa by the continued presence of the French army.[9] Onwards from there, they were carried again into the economic system of the European Common Market, and became, willy-nilly, its overseas appendage.

For Africa, an area of weak economic bargaining power, it appears difficult to see the European Common Market as other than a guarantee of continued underdevelopment along existing lines. Arguing that unpopular case, an Ethiopian economist lately recalled what Alexander Hamilton had to say, in 1791, on the point of trade unification between weak economies and strong ones. "The United States," Hamilton then wrote, "cannot exchange with Europe on equal terms, and the want of reciprocity would render them the victim of a system which could induce them to confine themselves to agriculture, and refrain from manufactures. . . ."

This same economist concluded that the "consequence of such integrations between economies at different levels of development are exhibited today in north and south Italy and in the north and south of the United States. "Are we then going," he asked, "to perpetuate the North-South gap on a global scale?" This was what the European Common Market seemed likely to promote in Africa, and "a totally different type of arrangement would seem to be required."[10]

And thus it is that organic cooperation between African neighbors, a requirement for African progress so patently obvious that no one has dared to deny it in theory, has in practice been increasingly obstructed by a double barrier. This has consisted in the separatist interests of ruling élites, each of which has striven on the whole to defend its own separate hegemony, and, beyond that, in the divisive or dominating pressures of foreign systems whose overriding interest has lain in African disunity. Small wonder that experiments have made small progress.

All the same, the experiments are interesting. They help to illustrate the underlying trends, whether negative or positive. They illuminate this persistent if so often frustrated struggle to escape from the inherited situation. If the attempt at organic cooperation regularly fails, it continues to be made. And with each attempted making, the reasons for failure become a little more evident, better defined, while the conditions for success can be increasingly understood. And just how powerfully the old ideas of African unity have remained alive — of unity in diversity, no doubt, but of organic unity just the same — may be seen even in the lengthy list of plans and programs built around the concept of territorial reorganization.

It would be tedious to catalogue all or even most of these. Some were small in scope, or large but short-lived. Becoming politically independent in 1960, Senegal and Mali were federated but fell apart upon the rocks of rivalries and pressures both domestic and foreign. A little later, Nkrumah's Ghana tried to establish a free trade zone with its northern neighbor, the Volta Republic, only to be thwarted by the restrictions of Volta's Paris-dominated monetary system. There were other such attempts. All failed; the inherited situation proved too powerful for them.

Others have had a wider scope. In no small degree under the impulse of Nkrumah's rhetoric and Ghana's sterling reserves, conferences began to be held on a continental pattern. As early as the end of 1958 an "all-African peoples' conference" assembled at Accra, sounding with a new note of confidence not only the theme of intraterritorial struggle for political independence, extended also to the Belgian Congo and the Portuguese colonies, but also, and even more, the theme of interterritorial unity of effort. After 1960 there came a veritable tide of intergovernmental meetings and organizations as the new leaders, free at last to move around the continent and meet each other, deployed their skills in a new kind of diplomacy. These were feasts of talk after a long and solitary silence. Sides were taken, ideologies propounded, rivalries debated, advantages sought: above all, perhaps, new acquaintances made. Maybe it was the first time, on any scale, that West Africans became aware of East Africans, or vice versa: or that the peoples of the north were able to consider, at least in some degree, the plight of the peoples of the south, or again vice versa. All this usefully continued and, in 1963, culminated in the founding at Addis Ababa of an Organization of African Unity to which all the then independent states adhered almost at once, and were soon joined by others which achieved political independence.

The charter of this portentous body can be seen as Pan-Africanist utopianism at its most baroque and ornamental. Its verbally splendid clauses provide for all-

African organs of representation, government, security, commerce, investment, and the rest. Sir Hugh Clifford might have enjoyed another exercise in fatherly sarcasm if he had been there to conduct it: as it was, others have conducted it for him. Most of them have missed the point.

There can have been few leaders — perhaps none at all, perhaps not even Nkrumah — who really thought that the OAU could govern independent Africa, or that any of these grandiose clauses could come into effect, whether in 1963 or long after. What most of them were glad to accept was something that would have an immediate use; and, as events were to show, they achieved this in quite large measure. They were not averse, of course, to defining "the ideal," the maximum, the long-term goal: to provide Africa with a charter of unity which, however "visionary," might rise in men's minds above the rivalries and squabbles of the moment. Beyond that, and more to the point, they were ready for a continental forum which should be theirs, and should give them a means of solving at least some minor difficulties along their way.

Much was absurdly pretentious about the OAU, let alone unrealistic; much has remained like that. Its meetings have often degenerated into an unbearably tedious succession of prepared presidential utterances, the one more empty of content than the other. Here, if anywhere, natural gifts of oratory and diplomacy have at times run terribly to seed, or at other times blown into clouds and mists of meaningless activity. Of course one cannot really say that Africans have done much worse, in this respect, than other peoples in world assemblies.

In the perspective of actual situations, the apparent inefficacy of the OAU has concealed a sometimes useful work. Its framework has enabled the leading spokesmen of contending camps — like its component members, the OAU is nothing if not an élitist organization — to reach across the barriers of the inherited situation: barriers whether of language or religion, educational formation or political loyalty. It has helped to produce a certain climate of opinion about what ought to be and what ought not to be; and to use this climate of opinion for modest and yet helpful immediate purposes, as well as to establish a number of collective attitudes.[11]

The list of interterritorial disputes and difficulties that OAU mediation has settled or helped to settle is already quite a lengthy one: between Algeria and Morocco, Ethiopia and Somalia, the Congo (now Zaire) and some of its neighbors, Guinea and post-Nkrumah Ghana, and so on down the line. With all this there has emerged a certain experience and precedent, a habit of remedial action, that may prove useful in the future.

There has also emerged a principle of common action, even though honored often only in the breach, on large issues such as the further decolonization of Africa, whether in the Portuguese territories, Rhodesia, Namibia, or South Africa. As early as February 1964, the second meeting of the council of ministers of the OAU, assembled in Lagos, agreed to refuse overflight or transit facilities to aircraft and ships plying to and from South Africa, and this ban has since continued, obliging the South African regime to fall back on Portuguese facilities in Angola and the Cape Verde Islands. Measures were taken to set up regular channels of material aid to the movements of national liberation in these still colonial territories. Though meager, these measures have also had their effect, and have likewise continued, being again reinforced by resolutions at the 1973 annual conference of the OAU.

All this, in turn, has contributed towards making the African voice at the United Nations more unified and forceful than it could otherwise have been. By and large, the African grouping in New York has thus formed a diplomatic "mass of maneuver" which has repeatedly drawn energy from what can unite Africans rather than from what divides them. One needs only to consider the UN record on sanctions against Rhodesia,[12] on the condemnation of Portuguese imperialism, on South African racism, on the status of Namibia and on related issues, in order to see this constant pressure as being anything but futile. It has helped towards preserving a certain standard of decent behavior in the mess and muddle of our times; and to this extent it may even have improved the general trend and tone of world debate.

Even on issues of interterritorial organic cooperation and planning, the record is not altogether bare. Here, too, the targets have been usefully stated; and it may be vain to ask for more at this stage of events. Thus September 1964 saw the establishment of an African Development Bank with a subscribed capital of about £80 million. About half of this capital has so far come to hand, or had done so by the middle of 1971, and the bank has already made a dozen development loans to various countries. Little enough; yet perhaps a useful token for a different future, as and when that future may be realizable.

All such minor gains have been achieved against a powerful adverse current. Existing structures and relationships of a colonial type cannot possibly be made to fit within the aims and attitudes of African unity, if only because that unity calls for different structures and relationships. Here again the words of Alexander Hamilton ring down the years: "If Europe will not take from [America] the products of our soil, upon terms consistent with our interest, the natural remedy is to contract, as fast as possible, our wants of her." There can be few people in Africa today, or at least in independent Africa, who suppose that Europe takes from Africa the products of her soil upon terms consistent with Africa's interest. But to contract Africa's wants of Europe is precisely what the mechanisms now in place, buttressed from time to time by new mechanisms such as the Common Market, are designed to obstruct or entirely to prevent.

Once again one meets the contradictory nature of the situation. The ruling élites of the OAU may put their signatures to plans for African development and independence. Yet in their *national* guise and attitude they may well be more persuasively attached to their separatist interests and positions, and to their partnership with external systems whose concern is to delay rather than promote unity. The general interest and the group interest, as ruling élites in "developed" countries have so often shown, tend to be loyalties that are mutually exclusive.

Hence, for example, the lukewarm support for liberation movements that are active in countries still colonial. The governments of the OAU have waxed eloquent in their support; yet not a few of them have found the revolutionary aspects of these movements a good deal more than distasteful. Some of them have openly preferred a diplomatic surrender to Pretoria or Lisbon, believing or at least arguing that this must be a better way to progress than boycott or other means of hostile pressure. Their further thought, it seems, is that acceptance of South Africa would also be a help towards conserving and promoting the economic status quo to which they are themselves attached. Thus Ivory Coast President Félix Houphouët-Boigny, arguing for "dialogue" between the OAU and South Africa, even went so far as to claim that "the whites of South Africa, who are Africans as much as the rest of us, have an outstanding role to play in the development of our continent, in peace and harmony. . . ."[13] A suprising claim, perhaps; and yet a logical one in Houphouët's mouth. Evidently a white South African capitalism can do for southern and central Africa, on this admittedly very conservative view of things, what a French capitalism can do for the Ivory Coast. And as Houphouët believes that the latter represents development, why not the former too?

The dialogue, as it happened, never got off the ground. One of its chief sponsors, Dr. Kofi Busia of Ghana, was removed from power by men who rejected the proposal; other leading spokesmen of the OAU condemned it for a variety of reasons; President Houphouët changed his mind on the usefulness of pressing it further. This was another of the minor ways in which the OAU has reflected an underlying consensus of opinion about the future of Africa.

If it is true, for all these and comparable reasons, that continental unification on a rational and federal plan remains a matter for the distant future, what about less ambitious plans for regional cooperation? Two illustrations may be helpful.

One is that of ex-British colonial East Africa: the territories of Kenya, Uganda, and Tanganyika (which became Tanzania, having federated with Zanzibar in 1964). As long ago as 1917 the first two of these territories were brought within a customs union to which Tanganyika was added after World War One and imperial Germany's defeat. The union provided the framework for an East African common market which, from early in the 1920s, was aimed more or less consciously at protecting and fostering the white-settler economy of central Kenya, and especially the infant industrial base that was to be created in Kenya's capital, Nairobi.

When independence came, early in the 1960s, the new governments took over this framework in order that each could benefit from a larger domestic market than its own national territory. They hoped to make it an exemplary regional unification, articulating cultural and political autonomies within a system of interdependent economic ties and common interests. It was a kind of union, however, with disadvantages for the relatively weak. The relatively weak in this case were Tanganyika, and to a lesser extent Uganda. They soon found that the lion's share of advantage was going to the relatively strong, in this case Kenya; and that Kenya's advantage was growing rather than diminishing. They discovered, for one example, that hydroelectric power produced in Uganda was being sold to Kenya at rates which were actually cheaper than those charged inside Uganda. If net benefits of some £17 million a year were being realized from the common market, almost all of this was accruing to Kenya, while Tanzania, by the middle 1960s, appeared actually to be losing two or three million a year; and meanwhile fresh investment poured into Nairobi by foreign interests eager to exploit the Kenya preferences they could thereby gain.[14]

It was, of course, what some have prophesied will happen within the European Common Market. Given existing structures and relationships, capital gains flow from the relatively rich and developed to the relatively rich and developed, not to the relatively poor. So existing developmental contrasts will tend to be continually enhanced. This was what was already happening within the East African common market. Since 1965, especially under Tanzanian pressure, efforts have been made to correct this inherent imbalance of gain. A commission on East African economic cooperation was formed under the chairmanship of a former Danish minister of finance; and in 1967 its work duly led to a formal treaty of revision. A redesigned East African Economic Community began to take shape, and provision was made for eventual membership by inland neighbors such as Zambia, Burundi, and Rwanda.

Further progress will obviously depend on further reconciliation of territorial economic interests. As it stands today, the treaty does apparently correct most of the discriminations that worked in Kenya's favor. But its potential will clearly rest on new departures which do more than reform existing structures and relationships. There is at present, for example, a divergence between

Kenya policy, generally favorable to foreign private enterprise, and Tanzanian policy, generally opposed to that, which may yet prove too strong for reconciliation.

On the other hand, new initiatives by the Tanzanian and Zambian governments of Presidents Nyerere and Kaunda already contribute to a greater regional cohesion. These include an oil pipeline from the Tanzanian coast to the Zambian copperbelt; an all-weather road linking Dar es Salaam with Lusaka; and, likely to count for most of all, a similar link by railway that was nearing completion under Chinese construction in 1974.

Another illustration, this time from West Africa, throws light on other obstacles in the way of rational cooperation within a regional framework.

The river Senegal measures nearly 1,100 miles from source to sea, rising near the inland frontier of Guinea and flowing through Mali to become the frontier of Senegal with Mauritania. French surveyors long ago proposed that a proper management of the waters of the Senegal, whether for hydroelectric power, river transport, irrigation, flood control, and other purposes, could be of much benefit to all four countries. As it is, the Senegal has remained a largely unexploited river. Though it falls fairly rapidly for its first four hundred miles, the Senegal produced no hydroelectric power till a recently completed dam on the Senegalese sector, where the fall is very slow, began producing some a little while ago. And while its lower course is navigable for shallow-draught vessels as far inland as Kayes, or nearly six hundred miles from the Atlantic, this is possible only for two or three months a year. Swelling in the rainy season, this great river shrinks sadly in the dry, and might not even manage to reach the sea were it not for the action of ocean tides along its estuary.

The last years of the outright colonial period saw some preliminary research and planning. Then in 1963, after independence, a four-state committee was formed for the Senegal river basin. This committee was assured of some financial support, from UN sources, upon the reasonable condition that all four states should agree about its use. But that, of course, was where the shoe pinched. Guinea had little direct interest in preferring this or that proposed scheme, but Mali backed a dam in one place while Senegal backed a dam in another, and Mauritania pressed for priority on improving irrigation by other means.

To these territorial divergences, more were added. Guinea had acquired independence in the face of bitter French hostility and boycott; Senegal, Mali, and Mauritania had done so while retaining strong links with Paris. Senegal became a leading member of the French-projected OCAM, or Common Organization for Africa and Madagascar, a platform for the greater glory of Marianne that gave its orators, notably President Senghor, some of their finest opportunities for rhetoric, but otherwise served for little but to reinforce the neocolonial status quo. The Guinea government of President Touré, then under more or less continual attack from Marianne and her admirers, not unnaturally resented OCAM. Mali radicalism tended to support the same resentment till 1968, when a pro-Paris coup returned that vast savannah country to the fold of francophone orthodoxy. Another sharp dispute, again between Guinea and Senegal, arose in the wake of the Portuguese-propelled raid on the Guinea capital and President Touré's life in November 1970.[15] Agreement on what to do about the Senegal river remained far to seek.

Since then the whole scheme seems to have hung fire, while the Senegalese government have gone ahead with their own dam at Dagana. Does this reflect a hopelessly endemic disunity? The answer is ambiguous. Influences powerful within the status quo were now casting about for new formulas and frameworks. So far these small states of the old French West African colonial federation, of Afrique Occidentale Française or AOF as it was universally called, had continued to exist within the overall French monetary and political sphere. Yet they had done so separately, with each governing group in rivalry with other governing groups. Wasn't it time, perhaps, to re-create AOF in a new guise of political independence? Wouldn't that be more rational, more convenient, a stronger defense of the established order? In 1970 there was proposed, actually in Bamako, the capital of Mali, a new kind of AOF, the Communauté Economique de l'Afrique de l'Ouest (CEAO).

The idea was not exactly new. As long ago as 1959, even before independence, four of the territories of the old colonial federation (Ivory Coast, Dahomey, Niger, and Upper Volta) had been joined in an "association" known as the Conseil de l'Entente; and Togo made a fifth in 1966. Like OCAM, this Council was little more than an administrative means of easing the problems of separatist nationalism within the monetary and economic unity of the French-franc zone, and was otherwise a talking-shop. Overshadowed by the Ivory Coast, it had no life of its own. The new organization, CEAO, was to supersede it, being joined by Senegal, Mauritania, and Niger.

Had this come about as planned, CEAO would indeed have become a new-style AOF, with only Guinea as an odd man out. Then one might reasonably have said that Paris had come near to recovering its full economic hegemony of the outright colonial period, modified only by verbal changes and appearances, flags and national anthems, and by the wider but essentially similar arrangement of the European Common Market. The perpetuation of a balkanized West Africa would be confirmed in every basic way, and the chances of building a unity in genuine political independence would at least be long delayed. The liberation of francophone West Africa, in any sense meaningful to the development of people as distinct from the growth of subordinate economies, would scarcely have begun.

But the gains of the political independence of 1960, however limited, were nonetheless real gains. They represented an emergence from subjection; and this is a fact of a kind that does have a life of its own. What this means is that the game is only in its opening phases. The record of this "new AOF," this West African Economic Community (CEAO), shows that too. For things did not fall out as planned. There were two immediate reasons.

In the first place, the sanctity of French culture has not been able to alter the facts of geography. The francophone states of West Africa are not alone, but neighbors of anglophone states, and the latter include two, Nigeria and Ghana, which are much weightier than or as weighty as any of the francophone units. At about the same time as CEAO was in gestation, these anglophone states were negotiating their own arrangements with the European Common Market. Their eventual success was obvious, and became certain with the forthcoming entry of Britain. So it became similarly certain that CEAO would either wither away, like the Conseil de l'Entente before it, or develop into something notably different from the old AOF, for it would have to envisage inclusion of the anglophone states. This prospect put the cat among the francophone pigeons for a while, and led Presidents Senghor and Houphouët-Boigny, the African architects of CEAO, into producing a "by-stages" formula.

Secondly, not all the francophone states enjoyed the idea of living forever as satellites of Ivory Coast and Senegal, themselves satellites of Paris. North of Nigeria, the republic of Niger began to see that cooperation with Nigeria, outside the French-franc framework, might be very helpful. So did Dahomey and Togo, the latter even going so far, in May 1972, as to form with Nigeria an embryonic "Common Market" of their own. For Dahomey the lesson was even clearer; with about half its population sharing a language with its immediate Yoruba neighbors in Nigeria, a close cooperation with Nigeria appeared increasingly attractive. When CEAO was formally inaugurated at Abidjan, capital of Ivory Coast, early in 1973, Dahomey and Togo accordingly stayed out, and Niger went in only with misgivings. The new-style AOF consequently started, at this "stage," with only six members: Ivory Coast, Senegal, Niger, Upper Volta, Mali, and Mauritania.

It remained to be seen what would now happen. In

the long run the hegemony of Paris would clearly give way to the weight and power of Nigeria and the small peripheral states which seem likely to come increasingly within the Nigerian sphere. Yet we live in a time when the old nationalisms of Europe also give way to the weight and power of new economic structures, and most notably of the huge transnational corporations in whose image the European Common Market has been formed. An AOF in new guise is clearly no longer possible. But what is still very possible is the emergence of an even wider West African "community" which will have the same essential economic relationship with the European Common Market as the neocolonial AOF has had (Guinea alone apart) with Paris.

If so, the basic restructuring of a politically independent West Africa will have entered a new framework of economic subordination. To return to our illustration, the Senegal river may then be developed by interterritorial cooperation, but it would be a development within a system interested only in the growth of what exists, and opposed to any systematic transition to the noncapitalist and eventually socialist structures within which a genuine and overall development of people and their resources can alone become possible.

That is what the present prospect indicates. Will it be realized? Here we reach great issues that pass beyond the limits of this book. As things stand, and seem likely to go on standing, the tremendous productive advances of the advanced capitalist countries over the past years have been purchased at a dual cost: that of a steadily widening gap in usable wealth, in living standards, between the "developed world" and the "Third World," and that of a deepening inflationary crisis within the "developed world." Will these negative factors of relative impoverishment lead to the "final crisis" of the whole system?

It would be rash to think so. A recent discussion of the question has suggested, for example, at least two ways in which the system may again solve its own inner contradictions. The first might be by way of market integration of Eastern Europe, under one or other political form and leadership, thus providing another large field for growth of what exists, and giving the system another large outlet for the surplus capital of its own growth. The second might be "by Third World specialisation in classical forms of industrial production . . . while the centre [i.e., the "developed" countries] reserves for itself the development of ultra-modern forms, such as automation, electronics, the conquest of space, the atom...."[16]

The "Third World periphery," on this view, "would accept another type of unequal specialisation." Under the old specialization, the "Third World periphery" produced primary products and materials while the "developed centre" produced industrial and consumer goods, giving rise to the widening inequalities we see today. Under the new one, the "level" would be raised: in a sense, much as the level of black wages can be raised in South Africa without changing the basic system: indeed, as a means of reinforcing that system. And thus "the unequal development of the world system would find a second wind."

These considerations suggest some other lessons of the current scene. For one thing, they emphasize the integrality between Africa's situation, between the whole "Third World's" situation, and the situation of the "developed" world. Africa's crisis — and the word is not too strong for the trends of today — is part of a general crisis, and in this general crisis the peoples of the industrially advanced countries are as much involved with the plight of Africans as Africans, willy-nilly, are involved with us. What we are watching is not some distant drama far divided from the comforts and concerns of Europe and America, even if that is how it may often seem to be: the drama is as much ours as theirs, and cannot be resolved at the "periphery" without calling into question the posture and prospects of "the centre." The two "situations" are interdependent, intertwined, inseparable in their causes and their consequences. If peace is indivisible today, then so is progress.

The example of the Portuguese colonies may appear extreme. Yet its very extremeness throws a sharp light upon the wider scene. If the peoples of the Portuguese colonies have had to defend themselves and their right to progress through a decade of warfare at its most destructive, this is because the people of Portugal have not been able to do the same, even though the consequences for most Portuguese are measured in a growing oppression and impoverishment. And such is the wretchedness of Portugal today that a solution for the Portuguese people, the ending of these wars in which they desperately suffer, seems far more likely to come from "the periphery," the victory of the Africans, than from self-help inside Portugal.

The linkage between "periphery" and "centre" goes obviously wider. For if the people of Portugal have not been able to defend themselves, save by flight abroad,[17] this is not only because of the police and military power of their own rulers. It is also and perhaps even more because Portugal is itself a "periphery" of the world capitalist system, which helps continually to bolster the Portuguese regime at home and protect it abroad.[18] So it is that a solution for Portugal is profoundly involved in the possibilities of change in the countries of the "centre." Again one sees how all these "situations" tie into and turn upon each other.

Which is not to say, one may repeat, that the "periphery" cannot solve its problems, or begin to solve them, without the "centre's" having done the same. If it were so, the African outlook would indeed be bleak. On the contrary, the Portuguese example very much suggests the reverse, the great likelihood now being that the "periphery," in this case the colonies of Angola, Guinea/Bissau and Mozambique, will embark on constructive change before Portugal does, and even that Portugal's chance of doing so will depend upon this progress in Africa. Only the destruction of its colonial system, in other words, may weaken Portugal's police state to the point of allowing democratic progress in Portugal to develop and succeed.

And it may even be that this "order of progress" — the "periphery" before the "centre" — will prove to be a general rule in the long perspectives of history, or, as Samir Amin has lately proposed, has in fact always been the underlying rule of historical change.[19] Or, putting it another way for this context, that "we" shall not "survive" unless Africa does. Which again is not to say that we shall be wise to sit back and merely contemplate the perspectives of history. Progress, like God, helps those who help themselves.

Another consideration is that Africa's present situation is necessarily unstable, and likely to remain so while a great and difficult transition gradually unfolds. We have glanced at some of the reasons for this instability: at the constrictive inadequacy of existing economic structures; the deepening contradictions between sectoral growth and overall "underdevelopment"; the similar contradiction between dominant groups or bureaucratic élites eager to exploit their chances, and their evident inability, given their enclosing circumstances, to grow into ruling classes and thereby consummate a bourgeois revolution in their countries. All this had led to frequent overthrows and upsets, and can do nothing else. All this has emphasized the inherent futility, in any case, of trying to make progress in Africa by continuing to build bourgeois nation-states during an epoch when such nation-states have ceased to be a means of progress anywhere else.

This is not to question, of course, the right of Africans to their own nationhoods, or that forms of organic and functional unity between peoples will not take a national guise, and even must take that guise. But this unity between African nations and within African nations cannot come about by means of the bourgeois nation-state. Even those who still think that it can, or those who tell the truth of what they think, soon find themselves denying it. "My idea of African unity," says President Senghor, "is the same as that of General de Gaulle: we must build an Africa of the fatherlands." Yet three years later we find the same President Senghor observing that

"African unity is not for tomorrow. . . . It will come only after we have vanquished the tribal hatreds, the micronationalisms, the rivalries for leadership, and all the divisions we have inherited from the coloniser of yesterday."[20] But isn't Senghor's "Africa of the fatherlands," like de Gaulle's "Europe of the fatherlands," precisely predicated on the basis of the bourgeois-nation state that begets and cannot not beget, least of all in Africa, those very micronationalisms which, according to Senghor, stand in its way? So it is that great men contradict themselves.

All too clearly, the struggle to escape from a colonial condition has to be long and arduous, and there can be little in the present scene that speaks of success. Yet to look at things as they really are is not necessarily to become pessimistic. Only those who know of no way out, who see no alternative but to fasten their every hope on some miracle within the present order of things, can be pessimists today. Indeed, they can be nothing else.

The optimists will look for signs of change, for underlying currents which divide away from acceptance of things as they are. They will consider how far a nationalism predicated on a quite different basis may be viable, and why it is that one of Africa's outstanding thinkers could remark, on this point, that "there are no real conflicts between the peoples of Africa. There are only conflicts between their élites. . . ."[21] They will weigh the changing balance of social forces in long-term response to the great movements of the past thirty years: to the vast growth of urban populations which become, more and more, urban proletariats; to the myriad tentacles of new understanding that now reach out to villages and hamlets long lost in rural isolation; to the consequences for thought and action that flow from Africa's being opened to the four winds of world experience; to the rise of generations increasingly freed from the preconceptions of the colonial and precolonial past. There will be plenty of reasons, then, for holding that a defeatist note would be false to the totality of facts and possibilities which have comprised, and continue to comprise, the African renaissance of our times.

We shall witness many more upsets and upheavals. But here again it would be the absence of upheavals that would justify pessimism, for their absence would spell acceptance of things as they are, and would signal a perhaps fatal relapse into the trends of overall impoverishment now in play. Then indeed one might well fear that the dismal record of many Latin American countries over the past hundred years was to be reproduced in Africa as well.

At the same time, just as clearly, we have to know how to distinguish: between those upheavals which are little or no more than outbursts of anger or dismay, of personal intrigue or group rivalry or foreign interference, and other kinds of upheaval, creative kinds, which arise from a serious effort to breach the enclosing framework.

CHAPTER FIVE

The Development of People

My apology for reviewing so wide a field is that one cannot usefully attempt to look at the basic problems in any other way. On the other hand, a mere catalogue of situations, trends, and statistics would remain no more than that; and a catalogue is of little use to constructive argument. What that calls for is interpretation. Now anyone familiar with this scene, so dense, tumultuous, and diverse, will know that its inner truth is nothing if not elusive. Many of its situations have turned over on themselves during the past twenty years, not once but several times, and even the apparently soundest of interpretations along the way have had to be revised. All the same, I offer some conclusions here as the harvest of long observation, and with the added confidence of knowing that I am not alone in having reached them.

There is today, then, the knotting together of a complex of problems which arise in no substantial sense from the inherent frailties of human nature, but wind up from a crisis of social institutions and systems. These last terms I use to indicate the dominant socioeconomic and cultural structures founded in those relations of production and exchange which now dominate life within Africa, as well as between Africa and the industrialized world. The crisis is therefore fundamental and inherent: it cannot be wished away, nor can it be removed by an effort to make these systems work better. Just as surely as its resolution will not bring utopia, so also a continued failure to resolve it will lead to disaster.

This progressive breakdown remains the accompaniment of the prolonging or modifying of structures taken over from the last period of outright colonial rule. Let me emphasize that I am not saying that these structures were merely imposed from outside, a merely exotic cage of ideas and institutions which could, as it were, be lifted away to leave a free ground for every option. On the contrary, they represent the product of all that long and various history of change and compromise evolved by Africans themselves, whether from their precolonial experience or in confrontation with colonial powers. So we are in the presence of a close and often tortuous interlocking of elements indigenous and foreign; and this weaving has been hard to unravel and understand.

Hard not only for us, but also for Africans. It was the emancipation of ten or fifteen years ago that made understanding possible; and it is above all in this chance of enlightenment, I suggest, that history will perceive the true victory of that emancipation. Having climbed the psychological summit of a regained self-rule, Africans could at last begin to see what they could scarcely have seen earlier: the traps in which they were caught by a persistence of late-colonial institutions and relationships.

This enlightenment has spread in the past few years, and the prospect that has now appeared is that palliative measures will fail. The modification or reform of what exists will not be enough. What exists, by and large, supposes an attempt at the impossible: at the building of indigenous capitalist systems in a world where no such new systems can any longer see the light of day. Useless to argue the precedents of Australia and its like, where new capitalist systems have been built in the present century and whose real sovereignty has become relatively large. The African states are in a different position. The most they can hope to do, in that direction, is build weak subbranches of great commanding systems, overseas, whose monopolies of power they could never challenge, and whose removal of their wealth they could never stop. In that direction they would be able to argue more effectively about the crumbs, but not about the cake.

Even their power to argue about the crumbs would dwindle, not grow. For an effort to build systems modeled on those of western Europe or North America — necessarily, that is, systems of bourgeois or parabourgeois nationalist rivalry — would further reinforce their disunity among themselves and, among other things, weaken their collective voice in world assemblies. Any such effort at building capitalism would suppose the continued rule of entrenched élites, in each country, whose very existence and mode of operation would remain, as today, condemned to incipient or actual conflict.

So it is that reformist nationalism, the nationalism of the great epoch of expanding capitalism, falls sadly upon its old age and decline. Powerful liberator though it was in the past, today it can repeat itself only in the angers of frustration or provincial farce. And this, one sees again, is where the African problem acquires its universal sense and meaning. Existing lines of policy and action can lead to no "take-off" in Rostow's sense or any other: rather do they lead to an ever-nearing crash. A viable Africa, an Africa in true development of its people, cannot now proceed from the growth of what exists, but only from a far-reaching change in what exists. Yet a far-reaching change in what exists concerns not only Africa, but also Africa's relations with the industrialized world. The problem, once more, is ours as much as theirs.

The point here, one may perhaps insist, is not that modification has no value, or cannot be useful in improving what exists: the point is that modification will evidently fail to get at the roots of "underdevelopment" and conflict. The short-term gains of modification are indeed very obvious. Over the past few decades the Africans have greatly influenced the course of their relationships with the rest of the world, and they have done this repeatedly out of the resources of their own thought and courage, self-confidence and capacity for original action. On a subjective plane, the gray conformity of colonial thought or absence of thought, or of any encouragement to think, has largely vanished from the scene. Objectively, much is better than before.

Consider, for example, a report that Julius Nyerere could offer, in September 1971, on the first decade of Tanzania's independence. "It would appear from an analysis of the census figures of 1957 and 1967"—and he was careful to underline their poor reliability—"that the average life expectancy at birth has gone up from something like 37 or 38 years to something like 41 years"; and that, while "infant mortality was between 200 and 250 per thousand live births in 1957, [it] is now between 160 and 165 per thousand live births."[1] Similarly, whereas in 1961 forty-seven mothers in every 10,000 died in childbirth, the figure for 1967 was said to be down to about twenty-seven.

A large incidence of smallpox has given way to a small one; the same appears to be true of polio. Better health services have had their good effect. Opened in 1963, a medical school at Dar es Salaam now has an intake of between thirty and forty students; and this will soon be much larger. In 1961 Tanganyika had only twelve doctors of its own; ten years later there were 123. Fourteen nursing schools in 1961 produced 235 nurses every year; twenty-two schools now turn out an annual 422, and better trained as well. In 1961 Tanganyika had twenty-two rural health centers; in 1971 there were ninety.

Schooling has expanded, again as in many African countries. In 1961 Tanganyika had 11,832 pupils in secondary schools, but only 176 were high school seniors. Ten years later, the comparable figures were 31,622 pupils and 1,488 seniors. Education has improved in size and scope; so have teaching curricula, and teaching itself. For example, none of the schools of 1961 taught, or was capable of teaching, the history of Africa in any of its phases save that of the colonial period, and even this was done from a colonialist standpoint. Today, by contrast, both primary and secondary pupils read African history from an African standpoint with texts specifically framed for this purpose, and with teachers trained in the subject.

The improvement of what exists can be seen in other fields. Over the first decade of Tanzania's independence, cotton production more than doubled; so did that of coffee and pyrethrum; sugar production actually trebled. All this has led to the familiar picture of rising exports of cash crops: in 1970 Tanzanian exports were worth about 73 percent more, in money values, than in 1961. Processing and manufacture also made some progress. President Nyerere reported on the same occasion that the proportion of imports accounted for by consumer goods fell, over the ten years, from 45 percent to 9 percent, while the import of capital goods rose from a proportion of 31 percent to 53 percent. Tanzania, in other words, was in process of getting a better long-term value from her exports. These, for the first time, begin to open the way to forms of development that are manifest, for example, in the expansion of electricity supply from 144 million kwh in 1961 to 380 million ten years later.

At a first glance, then, the results of a decade may even suggest that a continued modification of what exists can still do the job. But this is an impression, whether of Tanzania or any other African country, that will not hold. Modification of what exists may provide valuable improvement of the immediate situation. What it does not do is match these with structural changes which can lead to overall development.

This is what Mr. J. H. Mensah, Ghana's economics minister in 1970, was getting at when he deplored the 1960s as a wasted decade: what Ghanaians had done in those years, as he put it, was to build a modernizing infrastructure without building the means to pay for it.[2]

Putting it in another way, one can say that the concept of élitist growth, the policy of growth-of-what-exists becomes increasingly at war with the concept of true development, with the policy of growth of communities-as-wholes. Here, more than anywhere else, lay the governing circumstances of Nkrumah's failure after 1961: there arose in Ghana a deepening conflict between the few who prospered and the many who did not, between rising standards of living of the people at the top and stagnant or even declining standards of the people at the bottom. In this, nothing was changed by Nkrumah's fall, if only because the men who then followed him were themselves convinced, as he was not, of the virtues of élitist rule.

Nyerere and some others have taken a different view. "During 1966," he recalled in his report of September 1971, "there was a gradual realisation that . . . the nation . . . was drifting without any sense of direction." There was confusion of policy and aim; growing discouragement; "an increase in the amount of inequality between citizens;" resentment at privileged beneficiaries; and a general trend towards waste of funds in luxury consumption. "The country was beginning to develop an economic and social élite whose prime concern was profit for themselves and their families, and not the needs of the majority for better basic living standards."[3]

These were the superficial signs of a deeper disarray. It was becoming clear that "economic growth in statistical terms is not synonymous with development in people terms."[4]

The very successes of the reformist programs of the previous ten years were now seen as threatening the chances of further progress. Better social services were producing needs and expectations on an upward curve of demand which the productive system must increasingly fail to satisfy. This inflationary "scissors" between needs or expectations on one hand, and possibilities of·satisfying them on the other, could be seen dramatically in the plight of students leaving school at the completion of their studies, especially among those who left at the end of the primary stage.

During the late colonial period, a youth or young woman who completed primary school looked for white-collar or other "respectable" and urban employment, and was persistently encouraged in this by the colonial ethos: he or she, however little instructed, was said to be an "educated native," and, as such, a member of society. This tradition, if one may call it so, has continued. But the improved standards of African schooling since independence have made it much harder for the primary-school leavers. Every year, nowadays, the labor market is assailed by a growing number of secondary-school students whose qualifications far outshine those of their humbler competitors. Neither category can find all the jobs it needs, or, rather, the kind of jobs it looks for; but it is obviously the primary-school leavers who suffer the larger frustration. In Kenya, for example, the year 1970 brought 200,000 new primary-school students into the labor market. But this was only a beginning: the following years, it was feared, might even raise the annual total to 500,000. And there are few African countries that do not face, in one degree or other, exactly the same conflict between social and economic structures.

These young men and women with primary schooling

are, of course, the very persons upon whom far-reaching changes in social, cultural, and economic life ought to depend, for it is through them, above all, that new ideas and modes of action could be channeled to the most distant rural areas. Instead, they crowd into the towns, even though the towns cannot give them employment. Only a different ethos — stemming from a different set of social values, arising in turn from a different structure of society — can now turn them to the tasks that are waiting in the villages. The reigning ethos of the "private fortune and career" can only enlarge an already serious disarray.

With this ethos, moreover, set as it has been within other of the élitist-orientated policies of the 1960s, more education has repeatedly widened the gap in interest and action between the literate few and the preliterate many. Secondary and university education may have grown from little to more; the vast majority still have no access to education of any kind. In Tanzania, to continue this example, the crucial field of adult education for literacy was left quite untouched, if only because it could show no profit to policies which saw the future in terms of an élitist leadership concentrating on the crystallization of a property-owning class. Only in 1969 were efforts launched to right this. Then, by mid-1971 but now with different policies at work, upwards of three-quarters of a million adults were being organized in literacy classes and other kinds of schoolwork.

The lesson has been clearest, perhaps, in the sphere of land usage. Like other ex-colonies, Tanzania was at once thrust into a continued policy of economic growth by export of cash crops; and not, as we have just seen, without success. As elsewhere, however, this success rested little on higher productivity, but much on bringing more land under cultivation. The country's farmed acreage probably expanded by as much as 25 percent during the decade, and may continue to expand for some years yet. There was a little improvement, here and there, in productive methods. But this growth of cash-crop production took place, on the whole, within the same productive system as before. The system grew; but it did not develop.

For a time, it may continue to grow. Yet the population is growing at a rate much faster, and may be doubled in size by the year 2000. How will these human riches then be used? What will they eat? Expansion of export crops, under existing circumstances, tends towards a relative stagnation in food crops. The likely consequences are not hard to estimate.

Other examples point the same way. It appears possible to expand the existing system, but not in such a way as to ensure any significant improvement in the general standard of living. Growth may be palliative, just as are money grants from abroad, or maize in times of famine; but it can never be more than that, and it can be *that* only in diminishing degree.

These are hard sayings; but the truth here is a harsh one. Higher all-round standards of living can proceed only from the development of higher productivity in food production, and thus from profound social and cultural changes. Yet any such changes can in their turn proceed only from a break, necessarily a radical break, from the inherited situation, whether traditionalist or colonialist. This implies a break or series of breaks, comparable in scale however different in kind, with the consequences of the industrial revolutions of Western Europe and North America.

Certainly, different in kind. "Developed" policies of growth have placed the *summum bonum* at an infinite supply of consumer goods, whether they be motor cars at one end or bombing planes at the other. That sort of objective has been offered, as conceivably realizable, to small minorities in black Africa. Insofar as its realization is in any case possible, this must just as surely happen at the cost of social peace and civic freedom.

The development of people, as distinct from the growth of things, calls evidently for objectives which do not lie within the reach of the inherited situation, but which turn away in new directions. To draw the rural millions into new methods and relations of production, and into far more intimate forms of social and political participation; to bring purposive because self-imposed order into the confusion of ideas and attitudes which now animate the newly urbanized multitudes; to raise structures which can revolutionize the social consciousness of all these peoples; while exploiting the technology and skills of science, cooperation, and manufacture; to resolve the contradictions between ethnic separatism, however valid or valuable, and regional or even continental forms of unity, functional unity, such as can alone establish a solid basis for overall socioeconomic expansion; and to do this by a synthesis in which constituent parts and totality may be composed in a sufficient harmony: these are the kind of objectives which, more clearly now with every year that passes, begin to be seen as essential to human development here.[5]

The beginnings of an attempt to break sharply from the ideas of the inherited situation came. in Tanzania with the projection of a new policy, or rather of a new basis for policy, early in 1967. This was the Arusha Declaration of President Nyerere. Its fundamental thought was that the Tanzanian ruling party and government must now turn away from concentration on the growth of things, and concentrate instead on the development of people. This did not imply any lack of further interest in the growth of things, a luxury that a country as ill-equipped as Tanzania cannot possibly afford. But this growth should be promoted only within policies framed for an overall social development.

There followed three years of what Nyerere has called "questioning, defining and agreeing on the kind of nation we want to build." Meanwhile, so as to secure control of the economy, measures were passed to take banks, insurance companies and export-import businesses out of the hands of their foreign owners, and to bring them under national ownership as state or parastatal enterprises. New guidelines were laid down for policies of mass literacy and schooling, for rural cooperation of a modern type, and for industrial development. The familiar practices of relying upon foreign grants and loans for the financing of new projects, and of seeing development as essentially dependent on such grants or loans, were roundly condemned; and objectives of "self-reliance," of independent development, were set up and were discussed at least within the narrow circle of those round Nyerere who stood at the head of the ruling party and government.

"It is stupid," the new policy declared, "to rely on

money as the major instrument of development, when we know very well that our country is poor. It is equally stupid, indeed it is even more stupid, for us to imagine that we shall rid ourselves of our poverty through foreign financial assistance rather than our own resources." Yet this was just what men in authority *had* imagined. Duly encouraged by foreign advice, their essential idea about national development had been to draw up a list of desirable projects, of things that modern countries were thought to need, and call this a "plan." The task then was to tout it round the world till the necessary "aid" was raised. Usually the totals that were raised fell a long way short of what was asked. But even what was raised then flowed into a system which belonged in all essentials to the colonial period. Such moneys flowed, that is, into an élitist structure concerned with its own enlargement, rather than with overall development for the mass of the population.

This is not the place to attempt a review of Tanzanian affairs since 1966. The setbacks are obviously many, as they must be, and the outcome far from sure. Only a handful of Tanzanians could show much working grasp of what the Arusha policy was intended to mean. Some took it seriously; others thought it quite unrealistic, even if they did not always say so. This or that group in government or party pushed one way; others pushed against them. Peasants found it hard to understand that something new had happened, or must now be made to happen; administrators found it no easier to enlighten them, being for the most part little enlightened themselves. Beneath the surface of ostensible agreement, a "silent class struggle" went on between those who saw the future in terms of their own careers or the preferment of their group, and those who saw it in terms of revolution or at least of systematic change towards a new society.[6]

Yet the progress has been visible as well. A number of institutional changes have gone fairly well; the nationalizations have generally succeeded. Reliance on foreign aid has diminished. In the years 1961–1966, the annual average contribution of foreign aid to infrastructural projects had stood at about 44 percent. In 1967-1971, it fell to an annual average of about 26 percent, even though this was a period of major improvement in long-range communications and of several large contributions to the economy. The "ties of dependence" on foreign interests were reduced.

Meanwhile one can usefully look at other aspects of historical importance. To begin with, it may be argued, the language of the Arusha Declaration of 1967 signaled the first real attempt to state the problem of structural change, of revolution in the sense that I have been using here, in terms applicable to an African situation. Perhaps the language still suffered from a certain confused idealism. Nyerere, its *fons et origo,* has since then deepened his analysis and produced other formulations of a form and content more evidently realist. Which means, of course, more evidently socialist in approach: anyone who would wish to formulate a policy of true development — that is, of systemic change — will be forced to abandon the ideological conceptions of capitalism. And the alternative will at least point in a socialist direction: because, if it is a real alternative, it cannot point in any other. So it is, in Nyerere's thought, that one finds the steady development of ideas from an utopianist idealism in the early 1960s to an increasingly socialist analysis of reality, and, flowing from this, to a sharpening definition of the route that this alternative must follow.

The inherent difficulties are obviously immense. Leaving aside the distractions of "African Socialism" and the like, it remains that nobody agrees or even securely knows what a socialist society may really be. The blueprints are many and the models not few; but the thing itself can still seem far to seek. Christopher Columbus sailed for the New World and claimed to have found it, but what he really found were the islands of the Caribbean, and greatly to their cost. Sailing for socialism we are all discoverers now, but discoverers who are likely to be wary about being sure of having reached that necessary destination. What Tanzania has today is not socialism nor anything near it. The campaign launched at Arusha, and afterwards continued, was and is an effort to forge an overall development that shall be noncapitalist in organization and ethos, and therefore nonélitist; which proclaims socialism as its ultimate objective; which meanwhile aims at promoting attitudes and structures compatible with that objective; and so, expectably enough, is plunged in difficulties of comprehension or dissent. Its experience in these respects is repeatedly illuminating of the wider scene as well as of its own.

A different system of production has to suppose a different organization of people. After 1967, accordingly, official policy began urging those rural people who lived in isolated hamlets or homesteads to leave their solitudes, and to come together in self-regulating cooperative villages; and this change began to happen. By June 1971, there were thought to be as many as 2,700 new cooperative villages enclosing some 840,000 people. Since then, the total may be well beyond one million, or rising towards a tenth of the whole rural population.

But a different organization of people must also suppose the emergence of a different consciousness of needs and possibilities, collective aims and purposes, and with this, corresponding changes toward a different culture. It is a point upon which African thinkers have much insisted during recent years. Here in Tanzania, numerically, the start was impressive. But it collided with two obstacles in the inherited situation, each of them related to the existing level of consciousness.

One of these was what may be politely labeled as "bureaucratic deformation." Energetic officials, ambitious for their targets of persuading so and so many people to move from homestead to village, gave administrative orders rather than patient explanation, even though patient explanation was vital to the whole purpose of the move. Such officials tended to mount their Land Rovers and visit hamlets and homesteads in the bush and tell their people: "This is what we have decided. This is what is good for you. And the transport will be here next week." Here was a familiar case of "orders from above," another inheritance from the attitudes and systems of the past.

That misunderstanding was tackled and dealt with as well as it could be. But the inherited situation was also present in a more obstructive guise, drawing its persistence from ancient custom and tradition. People moved from homesteads into cooperative villages and found no difficulty, or so it appears, in accepting the ideas of cooperation; after all, they had long known these ideas in the elementary form of mutual aid among themselves. But if they took with them an acceptance of cooperation, they also took along their old methods of work and attitudes to work, partly out of peasant conservatism and partly because they knew no other. This being so, the whole experiment soon came under severe test and strain.

Government put in new water points and deep wells, more roads, new schools and clinics, staffing the latter as well as they could. Yet productivity still could not rise unless methods of production also developed. Short of that change, the gain from gathering isolated families into villages might be little more than a convenience for emergency, enabling hand-outs of food to be made more easily in times of want or famine. Since 1967, Tanzanian policy has therefore concentrated or been aimed at concentrating on the development of farming methods within this new cooperative relationship.

Yet theory and practice are stubbornly two things, not one; and in this respect, too, the resultant picture proved to be a mixed one. Thus the oxen-plow was encouraged; one could even say that it was introduced. In 1970 there were about 12,000 such plows in use throughout the country. This was still a small number, and that was understandable.[7] But it was also disappointing. "It ought by now to be a common sight in our countryside," Nyerere was observing in his report of 1971, "to see *ujamaa* [cooperative] village members, or even individual peasants, doing their ploughing and harrowing [with new tools]. But in most areas all that we see are people with backs bent under the hot sun, breaking the land with heavy hoes just as their ancestors have done for centuries." The different organization of people had yet to be reflected in a different system of production.

These examples lead to the heart of the problem of structural change in the "underdeveloped" countries. A strong assertion of independence by way of the nationalization of banks and other such institutions may be a necessary prelude to structural change. Yet no amount of change in the relatively advanced sector of the society in question, however advisable this may be, can produce much more than a bureaucratic organism, *unless* such change is embraced within a new cultural enlightenment across the whole society. And this kind of enlightenment, gateway to the different organization of people just as it is also the product of that different organization, cannot proceed from a bureaucratic organism, cannot be imposed from above, cannot be determined for the many by the few.

All this, at our time of day, may seem terribly obvious and yet still worth repeating. The enlightenment which can alone produce a new society arises first among the few, but to be effective it must flower and make its impact among the many. Short of that, the few will substitute their understanding, and therefore their authority, for the will and wisdom of the many; and then, as the twentieth century has more than amply shown, the time may come when the one will substitute his understanding, and therefore his authority, even for the will and wisdom of the few.[8]

A revolution that continues as well as begins by means of a "substituted" understanding and authority is one that stops, and must stop, halfway. Either it stagnates or else reaction gathers to overturn it in one guise or other, and then its original purposes can be saved only by another revolution, this time "at the base." In the deepest sense, no doubt, that is how things have to be, for the underlying dialectic of society, of any society, can work in no other way than by repeated change, so that this is saying no more than that every revolution is a process, like history's own unfolding, with no "final results" or "finished problems." Thus every great change is only a step along the road of mankind's further liberation, and must, in order to bear its full fruits, itself in due course be overcome and left behind. Even so, there remains a vast difference between the nature of social change conducted by means of "substitution" and of change conducted by the widening authority of understanding and participation "at the base." It is a difference on which the history of our century has taught some stiff lessons.

Every great change is subject to its own specific conditions of practice and possibility, whether objective or subjective, whether of internal or external pressure. The Africans have to make their saving revolution under conditions which are extremely difficult in both respects. Subjectively, they have to win through a jungle of inherited or implanted obstacles; objectively, they have to face a grim array of contrary pressures.

This is the background that explains why the Tanzanian attempt has attracted such wide and vivid interest in many quarters.[9] For here it is not only, and not even chiefly, that government and party have promoted changes "at the centre" by the nationalization of banks and other commanding heights of the country's economy. These were necessary to progress because they were necessary to independence of action. By themselves, however, they could only be a small step towards major social change: so long as they remained "by themselves," they might even become a backward step. They might then be seen as having "set the pace for the rise of economic bureaucracy . . . because managers, directors and administrators of parastatals [nonprivately owned companies] already constitute a formidable bureaucratic stratum."[10]

Far more interestingly and creatively, these changes "at the centre" were not allowed to remain "by themselves," but, as well, were enshrined in an effort to inspire and promote changes "at the periphery": changes in the organization and consciousness of Tanzania's great majority of rural people, nine-tenths of the whole population, by which alone a new society could be made to emerge. It is this effort which has endowed Tanzania's political situation with its general relevance as well as its particular importance, and has given its political leadership the characteristics of a movement of national liberation with all the gains, as well as the difficulties and setbacks, which this must imply.[11]

Within these brief limits, what other movements now suggest the same order of ideas, what other situations at present illustrate the "development of people" in Africa today? I should like to round off this inquiry with some notes on what is happening in the Portuguese African colonies of Angola, Guiné, and Mozambique.[12]

Here the story concerns nationalist movements whose immediate origins lay in the early 1950s, when their pioneers formed them, or their forerunners, in a necessary clandestinity. Thus the PAIGC (Partido Africano de Independência de Guiné e Cabo Verde: linking the mainland of Guiné with the culturally and historically connected Cape Verde archipelago) was formed in Bissau in August 1956; the MPLA (Movimento Popular de Libertação de Angola) was formed in Luanda in December 1956; while FRELIMO (Frente de Libertação de Mocambique) took shape in Dar es Salaam in July 1962 from a coalition of small groups formed a little earlier. Since then all three have greatly developed and enlarged themselves, and by 1970 were major factors not only inside their own countries but also in the wider African context.

These movements in the Portuguese colonies are in one sense eccentric to the main orbit of African nationalism, because they came into being and have developed in the generally uncharacteristic absence of any possibility of reform, and have consequently taken the path of armed revolt and resistance. This has given them a nature very much their own. It remains that they have shared the same challenges as other African modernizing movements elsewhere: they have had to operate, that is, within and against an inherited situation constructed historically by the imbrication of African life with the distortions of foreign rule. Their distinctiveness, no doubt, arises from response to the two governing characteristics of Portuguese imperialism: to its violence, which has led to African self-defense by counterviolence, and to its political immobility, which has allowed room for no serious attempt at modifying "what exists." In averting the distractions and confusions of reformism, this last has had an incidentally helpful consequence. Partly thanks to the absence of any chance of reform, the leaders of these movements have been enabled to see more directly and comprehensively where they and their peoples stand, and what they and these must do to save themselves.[13] For this, however, they and their peoples have had to pay a severe price.

The beginnings of their armed resistance came in the early 1960s, and were arduous and very painful. Since then, many different pressures have molded their practice and theory. The greatest of these pressures has been their need to survive and develop. This has meant that they have had to justify their policies not only to themselves but, above all, to the peoples they have led or sought to lead: to elucidate these policies, that is, not only as a necessary response to colonial misrule in the relatively short term but also, and more important though far more difficult to explain, as the necessary path to a new society after independence should be won.

They have thus developed from ideas of reform to ideas of revolution; but what is just as essential to understand about them is that they have not made this move gratuitously, or from merely doctrinaire or a priori prescriptions. If they had done that they could scarcely have survived, let alone developed, because no "imported doctrines" or "prescriptions" could long withstand the horrifying trials of guerrilla warfare under modern conditions. How, then, have they made this difficult but vital move in ideas? What are these ideas of revolutionary nationalism, and to what extent do they relate with the situations discussed earlier?

To begin with, as all their experience combines to show, the three movements in question—MPLA in Angola, PAIGC in Guiné, FRELIMO in Mozambique—can be said to have moved forward from reformism because they found nothing that they could try to reform.

The structures of traditional life offered nothing in themselves, or nothing in their political or parapolitical manifestations, save a "return to the past," whether in the form of a resurrection of lost chiefly or ethnic authority, or of messianic visions of a more or less comparable resurrection;[14] and none of this could provide the ground for any viable independence of a noncolonialist nature. Such manifestations had to be understood and absorbed; they could not be the program for a fresh start. Reform of Portuguese imposed structures, on the other hand, soon revealed itself as an even more hopeless enterprise. Even if actually possible, such reform could never lead towards or produce the different organization of people, the different consciousness of people, that were now required. It could lead only towards a form of neocolonial subjection.[15]

The best leaders of these movements, and they were fortunate in having outstanding men and women among them, accordingly began to work towards strategies of entire renewal. They began to find and to found democratic forms of organization of a type altogether new in these countries. They began to inspire these new types of self-organization with ideas and modes of action that could unite and illuminate all those who were now drawn into the struggle for one immediate reason or another. And all these, however bewilderingly various in their individual attitudes and approaches, began to acquire a sense of common purpose in the practical liberation of a new national community.

Although the 1960s were years of grim sacrifice, they were therefore also years of growing success. And gradually, as these leaders held firm to their principles and worked in these ways, they perceived that the practical definition and day-to-day meaning of the ideas of this liberation were in process of being bodied forth, as the pot from the potter's clay, by their on-going struggle for survival and expansion. This may sound solipsistic. Yet it is a description of an interplay between ideas and reality — as it were, between self and nonself — that provides the most valid explanation of why these movements, developing out of their own dynamics, have been able to win many advances, not least in the field of cultural progress. Because the making of a "revolution at the grass roots" can hardly be an obvious or easy one, and was not so here, it may be useful to enlarge on this.

A few determined persons can begin an armed resistance, a guerrilla counterviolence to the violence of misrule. That is relatively easy, and anyone who cares may adduce his own example. What is difficult is to continue.

For in order to continue it is necessary to win adherents. This in itself may be difficult: the mass of people among whom the "beginners" operate may be cowed by long subjection, confused by colonial mythologies, even very hostile to the perils of armed action. Even so, none of that constitutes the most difficult task which the beginners face. They may soon be able to win supporters: people who resent the status quo, who show good will to the guerrillas, who give them food and shelter and information about the enemy. But so long as the guerrilla group only wins supporters it will not develop, and it will scarcely even survive. Sooner or later, in every likelihood, it will be pinned down by enemy response and destroyed in isolation while its supporters melt away in fear or silence, flight or betrayal. Of this, too, the last dozen years have been rich in sad examples.[16]

What is necessary, in order to continue, is to win supporters who become participants and who participate in ways which continually grow and deepen, whether in action or in the enlightenment of a new political and social consciousness. Then indeed, as this difficult process is pushed forward, the guerrilla group will acquire reality as a people's movement, will put down strong roots, and, with continued sound leadership along the same lines, will pass beyond the point where enemy action can isolate and kill it. All the great examples demonstrate this process; most recently those of South Vietnam and its neighbors. And in their own place this is also how the movements in the Portuguese colonies have prevailed, and why, incidentally, the Lisbon propaganda argument, to the effect that these movements grow by forcing people into their ranks, is merely absurd.

The few, in other words, have to transfer their convictions, their ideas about the present and the future, their modes of understanding reality, *local* reality, to a sufficient number of the many. And a "sufficient number," in this context, means a number that grows continually in size and unity of action and consciousness. This the few can do only by entering fully into the concerns and interests of the many. All these things they must share and understand and make their own, while at the same time adding their own vision and understanding, so that the movement *moves* — but moves forward. Then it is that the ideas of liberation are identified and given strength, and, as the interplay continues, are endowed with specific form and application.

This transfer of understanding from the few to the many is a hard thing: in Amilcar Cabral's words, the hardest and most daunting thing of all.[17] The best of the leaders in the Portuguese colonies have succeeded in it by unfailing courage and patience, as well as by self-criticism and improvement of their methods. Under different conditions it is the central problem everywhere today. In Africa it is the same problem that TANU leaders in Tanzania have wrestled with in the case considered earlier, while other African countries with comparable aims among their leadership can furnish their various examples. If the examples in the Portuguese colonies are especially instructive and creative, this is partly because of the extremely severe tests and trials that the movements there have had to meet and overcome; and this is also the light in which their successes, like their failures, have to be measured.

Portuguese colonialism had long been notably reactionary and violent, reflecting in this the backwardness and behavior of the ruling groups or classes of Portugal itself. Over a prolonged period its effect has been to undermine indigenous institutions, morale, self-respect, and even the least hope of beneficial change. There is copious evidence of this long-imposed degradation, whether in Africa or in Portugal itself. For its consequences today, one need look no further than the colonial armies raised by Lisbon to fight alongside its own troops from Portugal. Tens of thousands of conscripted African soldiers, like tens of thousands of Portuguese, have continued to serve their imperial masters with more or less subservience, if with little enthusiasm, in the wars of Angola, Guiné, and Mozambique. Here indeed the old imperial policy of divide-and-rule has been applied with a ferociously destructive effect.

Striving in these circumstances for an entire renewal, and hence for a widening unity of thought and action, the leaders of these movements were themselves soon led, by the logic of their situation, beyond any program which was limited to mere reform of their countries' inherited situation. This was their great "point of change" when the fainthearts fell away or began to contemplate betrayal. But the majority, the men and women who mattered, stayed with the central lesson of their experience. If armed resistance were to be worthwhile, it must become far more than a revolt within any colonial framework or set of traditional assumptions.

Being sure of this, they came to see their policy as one of revolutionary nationalism. Within the "given" nationalist framework — one aspect of the inherited situation that could not be willed away — this meant a liberation from the past as well as from the present, clearing the way for a different future that would not deny the past but build creatively upon it. And then, though far from spontaneously, this revolution began to happen. Village people began to think new thoughts, act in new ways, and with an initiative and a style increasingly their own. Having looked for a new world, the leaders began to find themselves really living in it. What was happening was seen to impose and involve the remaking of all the attitudes and beliefs by which a people lives. Having won supporters who had become participants, and having passed the point where this widening mass of participants had become the heart and body of their organized action, these movements were now the instruments of societies which stood upon the threshold of great cultural change.

In 1970, seven years after the PAIGC had launched their armed resistance in Guiné but some fourteen years after they had begun their political struggle, this was how Amilcar Cabral described their cultural situation. "Consider," he said, "these features inherent in an armed liberation struggle: the practice of democracy, of criticism, and self-criticism, the increasing responsibility of populations for the direction of their lives, literacy work, the creation of schools and health services, the training of militants who come from peasant or worker backgrounds. . . ."

All these features of their struggle were inseparable from successful resistance and its political inspiration. But "when we consider these features, we see that the armed liberation struggle is not only a product of culture," a product of a people's effort to conceive and defend its own interests and values as a community, "but is also a *determinant* of culture. . . ."

And why? On one hand, "it requires the mobilisation and organisation of a significant majority of the population; the political and moral unity of the various social categories; the efficient use of modern weapons and other means of war" by peoples from a technologically primitive background. On the other, it likewise requires, because it cannot otherwise succeed, "the progressive elimination of tribal attitudes, and the rejection of social and religious taboos which inhibit development of the struggle: such as gerontocracy, nepotism, the social inferiority of women, as well as of rites and practices which conflict with the rational and national character of the struggle."

So it is, he concludes, that "armed struggle for liberation implies *a veritable forced march along the road of cultural change.*" In this struggle, any moment of success can have no wider value unless "it can be translated into a significant leap forward in the culture of the people *that liberates itself.*" Short of that kind of participation, self-liberating and self-enlarging, the efforts and sacrifices accepted during the struggle will have been in vain, and then the struggle, no matter how proudly bugled forth in claims of victory, will inwardly have failed.[18]

"A significant leap forward in the culture of the people that liberates itself," taking the word culture, as Cabral used it, in the widest sense of self-confidence and self-criticism: this then appears to be the central process now in play behind those remote frontiers. This is what the word "liberation" evidently means and why the meaning is revolutionary. For this is the development of minds, the development of people, into new and higher levels of awareness, explanation and understanding of themselves and their condition: the necessary prelude to the building of a new society, of a system of daily life that can eventually place these peoples on a footing of effective self-defense within the world as it is now. Alongside this kind of development, the mere business of warfare becomes little more than incidental.

Obviously, much else is also going on beyond those frontiers: mistakes and misunderstandings, individual failures or betrayals, momentary defeats, occasional and sometimes terrible losses, a daily toll of suffering that cannot be escaped except by surrender. Yet all this, like the actual warfare, is also in a real sense incidental. It is the development of people that alone matters in the long run; and the evidence for this was already very striking even by the early 1970s.

One recalls many examples. One thinks of the sharpening clarity and confidence with which the best of these leaders see and lead. Of the growing coherence of new ideas about unity and progress among peoples so sorely divided, and distracted for so long. Of collective cases: of individual cases: of the barely literate forest fighter who tells you his fruitless story of years of forced labor or of exile in the mines of South Africa, and then shows you his exercise-book scribbled with the conquest of a new knowledge, of a new power of understanding; and who then goes on to demonstrate, in the daily round of forest life, his capacity to explain what he is doing and why he is doing it; and who then again goes on to analyze what the enemy is doing and why the enemy is doing it, and who sets this off against his own conception of a sense of community within a nation struggling to be born.

It is in contexts such as these, not easy to observe yet still harder to describe, that these movements reveal their historical importance to an on-going emancipation from the past and the present. It is from this angle that one may see why Cabral has compared them with the coming of a new harvest, a harvest from long-hidden seed which now, maturing to fruition, brings cultural renewal and, with that, the prelude to a new life. "The culture of Africa's peoples springs forth again, across the continent, in struggles for national liberation."[19]

The language may sound romantic; its reality is not. Rather does it point to a development in political thought that signals a new phase, a postreformist phase, a post-populist phase that goes beyond the calculations and maneuvers of any short-term reformist operation, and carries the future within itself. Cabral was thinking of the movements in the Portuguese colonies, but he was also thinking in the wide and even continental framework within which struggles for this liberation, for this development of people, will take many different forms: often non-warlike forms, in the end only non-warlike forms. "But whatever forms they take, whatever their success or failure," these struggles "mark the beginning of a new era in the history of our continent; and they are, whether in form or content, the most important cultural element in the life of Africa's peoples" now.[20]

It is a statement, I think, that will echo down the years. Like most of what Cabral wrote, it points to a program for the future as well as for the present. Perhaps he would have found reason to modify its formulation, to deepen its meaning with the passage of the years ahead, and to give it still broader application; there is nothing to suggest that he would have found any reason to change its essence. Already, even before his assassination by a clutch of traitors in January 1973, his words were being reflected in the thought of others who worked in circumstances very different. It would be easy to demonstrate this by a full review of the African scene. Let me, in conclusion, revert for a moment to the case of Tanzania.

Early in 1971, grappling with its difficult and so far only initial effort to become a dynamic organization of

174

mass participation, instead of a mere vehicle of electoral acclaim, the Tanzania African National Union (TANU) embarked on its own "forced march" to cultural change. Central to this initiative was the issue and popularization of a small green-jacketed book called *Mwongozi* (*Guidelines*), a series of brief connected statements which say, in simple Swahili, what the development of people, as distinct from the growth of things, must really mean in the policy of party and government.

"For a people," says *Mwongozi*, "who have been slaves or have been oppressed, exploited, and humiliated by colonialism or capitalism" — the frame of reference, as you see, is as wide as Cabral's — "development means 'Liberation.' Any action that gives them control of their own affairs is an action for development, even if it does not offer them health or more bread. Any action that *reduces* their say in determining their own affairs, or running their own lives, is not development, and retards them — even if the action brings them a little better health and a little more bread."

To realize the force of these words, in their everyday meaning for everyday situations, one needs to recall the venerable tradition of ancestral conservatism, as well as the shorter but still long tradition of colonial authoritarianism. Each in their different ways have rejected every serious striving for social change. And their effect, as anyone might see, by no means ended with the hoisting of the flags of independence. On the contrary, it was prolonged in the minds and attitudes of many leading men and women for whom "development," as for their mentors overseas, continued to equal the mere growth of what exists, as though "more" is necessarily "better" irrespective of the conditions under which this "more" may be achieved. *Mwongozi* presents another view.

Conceiving development, at this stage of Africa's transition, as a mental as well as physical emancipation for the building of a new society which, in the measure of its emergence, will underpin and guarantee a continuing progress, *Mwongozi* goes on to state that revolutionary movements in independent countries, such as TANU aims to be in Tanzania, are "in fact, liberation movements." Almost echoing Cabral in his Syracuse lecture, given in New York to commemorate the Mozambican leader, Eduardo Mondlane, at the same time as *Mwongozi* was being written in Dar es Salaam, these guidelines claim that liberation movements, conceived in this sense, are in the van of Africa's political life. This was said in the immediate context of a call for better cooperation between parties such as TANU and the movements in the Portuguese colonies and in South Africa, Rhodesia, Zimbabwe, and Namibia; but it was just as clearly intended as a statement about Tanzania itself.

And it is easy to see why. By the end of 1971, to return again to the highly relevant case of the waGogo, some 200,000 of this ethnic group had left their homesteads and moved into grouped villages, expecting fulfillment of the government's promise to provide water, clinics, schools. Government was busy in trying to meet this promise, causing wells to be dug and land to be plowed and other services to be installed, if still on a minimal scale. Yet even if government were to do ten times as much, only half the problem of the waGogo would be solved. The other half would still lie in that process of cultural self-liberation which only they can carry through: grasping the opportunities that are now possible, calling upon their own initiative for new ways of working and of working together, making their "forced march" on the road of cultural progress, and, in so doing, raising their consciousness to the point where they see and understand the wider picture of their own situation within their country's situation, and their country's situation within the international one. It is to this other and far greater "half" of the problem that *Mwongozi* insistently points, and does so with the emphasis on adult literacy classes and village schools, on a new and democratic content of education, on rural clinics and health instruction for the many rather than "prestige hospitals" for the few, and, above all, on a call for popular participation in the political work of building a new society.

It seems to me that an attentive look at other countries would confirm the existence of comparable trends, however disguised or tentative these may be. They are not always manifestations of anything that appears like revolution. Yet they are certainly more than mere reform of what exists. That is the case, for example, with the present effort in northern Nigeria to displace traditional native authorities, emir-nominated and dominated, nonrepresentative in any democratic sense, ultimately dictatorial, by elective local councils. There again, as in many other cases up and down the continent, some obvious and others not, one can find a many-sided effort among previously voiceless or silenced people to achieve a new control over their communities, and to run their lives as they have not run them before, or even before thought it possible to run them, at least in remembered history.

But to place all this varied effort at the achievement of a broadly democratic authority in its full light, one needs to compare it with the reverse trend: with the effort to achieve new forms of authority by individuals or by hierarchical minorities. This is the trend we have looked at here, the trend towards the "middle-class solution," toward élitist and noncollective forms of authority. This is what Lisbon, for example, would now like to achieve: frustrated in the military field, that colonial authority would be happy to conceal itself behind another neo-colonial façade, and install its own apparatus of reforms. It could then appear like other such reformers, duly chanting songs of freedom and waving banners of democracy. Yet the *Mwongozi* of these reformers have a very different meaning from TANU's. Their principle rests on devolving responsibility from the top to the bottom, not the other way round, and very sparingly at that. And their solution, according to the examples we have lately seen in Africa (not counting those elsewhere!) and with no evidence to the contrary, is evidently no solution. It is only the prelude to yet another coup or comparable confusion.

If the general analysis proposed here is well founded, then one may perhaps begin to see the lines of thought and action along which Africa will find its answer to the troubles of today: to those fundamental problems posed by the general crisis of transition which confronts the whole continent, and which cannot be escaped. These lines indicate the rise of types of democratic but anticapitalist participation which will be new in form and content. They will be necessarily highly various in their detail and always hard to define, if only because they reflect a blurred and even tentative class-formation within societies which are still at an early phase of modernization and which, of course, have in many of their components a various history of their own development in the past.

Yet they are lines which converge. If the essential problem, as Cabral liked to insist, is for people to regain command of their own history, then the perspective now is that the continuation of Africa's history — as distinct from the continuation of Europe's history in Africa under a "native robe" — will turn upon the effectiveness of these new types of democratic participation whose outlines, and occasionally more than whose outlines, are already visible. No doubt it will be some time before they become clear and manifest, along with the interterritorial unities which they will promote. There will be no small number of those famous steps backward as well as forward. The significant locus of immediate progress will shift from one country to another according to the fortunes of the day. Increasingly, all this will be felt as a battle against time.

Will it sufficiently succeed? All that seems at present certain is that we stand upon the outset of a decisive period to be measured in decades and yet not in many decades. For the generations who will give the answer are already on the scene: more than half of the continent's existing population of today is under the age of twenty-five, and possibly even younger. These are the generations who must make their saving revolution, or see their continent reduced to an object of charity and worse. It is they who must find a route to a new society, to a different organization of people, to a different content of consciousness and will: by way of today's beginnings, by "the development of people," by the "forced march" to a new culture, and by all that these imply.

Notes and References

One. A Continental Crisis

1. The great theme-song of "development" in the 1960s, still much heard today. Cf. a characteristic appraisal of British policy for aid to Africa, sponsored by the official Overseas Development Institute: I. M. D. Little, *Aid to Africa* (London: Pergamon; New York: Macmillan, 1964), where, for example, we are told that what Britain should do is to "carry out a successful long-term development policy *for* other countries."

2. Report by David Martin, *The Guardian,* London, August 26, 1971; and for following quoted passage.

3. This situation was interestingly explored at the time in a series of articles in the weekly *West Africa,* for long a sharp critic of Nkrumah: see, for example, issues for January 18 and February 4, 1972. I have discussed it in its wider Ghanaian context in *Black Star: A View of the Life and Times of Kwame Nkrumah* (London: Allen Lane, 1973; New York: Praeger, 1974).

4. I have discussed this further in *The African Genius* (Boston: Atlantic-Little, Brown, 1969; published in London by Longman, 1969, as *The Africans*). See especially chs. 22–24. For a penetrating summary of West African economic situations and capacities before the colonial period, see early chapters in A. G. Hopkins, *An Economic History of West Africa* (London: Longman, 1973).

5. Some of these attempted solutions had characteristics of a late-mercantilist or "proto-capitalist" nature, notably in coastal or near-coastal regions of West Africa. Would they or could they have developed into indigenous capitalist systems if the colonial invasions and dispossessions had never taken place? It seems unlikely, if only because they acquired these characteristics within an international trading system that was designed to accumulate capital in Western Europe and North America, not in Africa. The colonial invasions were in this respect a logical succession to the Atlantic slave trade, which had already begun the process of "development of Africa's underdevelopment," and which, in every important sense, paved the way for the invasions. See also arguments in Hopkins, *An Economic History of West Africa*, ch. 2.

6. In 1973 a widespread famine in the plains of the western Sudan was popularly attributed to "a southward move of the Sahara," rather as though the great desert had not been gradually expanding for more than two millennia. The true reasons for this famine lay rather in the long-continuing failure to solve the problems inherent to Iron Age growth in a post-Iron Age period of "nondevelopment," i.e., of colonial and neocolonial stagnation. The same could be said of an even worse famine on the Cape Verde Islands in the early 1970s. This was attributed to the lack of rainfall. But lack of rainfall, as in the western Sudan, was nothing new and was only the immediate or contingent cause; the real cause lay in socio-economic stagnation or regression, especially during the past two decades. Another famine in Ethiopia, also in 1973, brought death to at least 100,000 peasants and their families. Once again, the disaster was attributable far less to natural causes than to the irresponsibility and incompetence of Ethiopia's ruling system.

7. M. J. Field, *Search for Security* (London: Faber, 1960), p. 29.

8. See D. L. Potts, *The Development of the Zambian Copper Economy*, 1928–70 (London: Longman, forthcoming). I have discussed these aspects in some detail in Part Four of

In the Eye of the Storm: Angola's People (New York: Doubleday/Anchor, and London: Longman, 1972, Penguin paperback, 1974).

9. The position is summarized by A. Ewing, *Industry in Africa* (Oxford: Oxford University Press, 1968).

10. Among writings of major importance in this crucial field of analysis, it seems likely that the first was the American Paul Baran's *Political Economy of Growth* (New York: Monthly Review Press, 1957). Other notable contributions, directly or indirectly relevant to the African situation, have been those of the Brazilian André Gunder Frank, *Le Développement du sous-développement: l'Amérique Latine* (Paris: Maspero, 1970; English translation, *The Development of Underdevelopment,* London and New York: Monthly Review Press); the Greek Arghiri Emmanuel, *L'exchange inégal,* (Paris: Maspero, 1969; English translation, *Unequal Exchange,* London and New York: New Left Review); the Englishman Michael Barratt-Brown, *After Imperialism* (London: Heinemann, 1963), and *Essays on Imperialism* (London: Spokesman, 1972); the Egyptian Samir Amin, *L'accumulation a l'échelle mondiale* (Dakar: IFAN; Paris: Anthropos, 1971), *L'Afrique de l'Ouest bloquée* (Paris: Minuit, 1971); *Le développement, inégal* (Paris: Minuit, 1973); and *Neo-Colonialism in West Africa* (London: Penguin, 1973); and others who have examined these or other aspects of the "development" issue, and have taken the debate further in one way or another.

11. Samir Amin, *L'Afrique de l'Ouest bloquée,* e.g. pp. 29–32 and ff.

12. Which is not to argue that palliative aid may not meanwhile be useful, even indispensable, in saving lives or suffering. Nor, still less, that foreign aid designed to help in changing "what exists" may not be very helpful. In the latter case one thinks, for example, of the aid being given by state or unofficial organizations to the liberation movements in the Portuguese colonies and English-speaking southern Africa.

13. See a large literature, and, for essential statistics:

Foreign Investment in the Republic of South Africa (United Nations ST/PSCA/SER. A.6, 1968); and S. Gervasi, *"Industrialisation, Foreign Capital and Forced Labour in South Africa* (United Nations ST/PSCA/SER. A.10, 1970). I have discussed the implications in *Which Way, Africa?* (London and Baltimore: Penguin, 3d ed. 1971), ch. 11.

14. The whole question of "spread effects" from colonial-type "booms" and "development" requires further investigation. On the available evidence, however, two conclusions appear difficult to refute. The first is that such "spread effects" occur only within the white-dominated and mainly urban sectors of such "dual economies," and are small. The second is that they are accompanied by a continuing pauperization of the majority of people living in the African-dominated and always rural sectors. See, e.g., R. B. Sutcliffe, "Stagnation and Inequality in Rhodesia, 1946–68," Bulletin of the Oxford University Institute of Economics and Statistics, 33, no. 1 (1971): 35.

Sutcliffe found, among other disturbing things, that between 1956 and 1968, a period much claimed by Rhodesian spokesmen as being one of continued economic development, "the ratio of white to black personal income per head has been virtually constant. In spite of much talk of African advancement, there is no evidence that more than a small fraction of the black population has seen any improvement in its relative economic position in 15 years of economic development." He concluded that economic growth in the urban sector, the white sector, also produced economic decline in the rural sector, the black sector. "The national income is progressively more unequally distributed because of the way in which it is earned and spent."

Analysis of the dual economies of the Portuguese colonies will yield the same conclusions. See my *In the Eye of the Storm: Angola's People,* Part Four; and footnote 8, Chapter Three, below.

15. For an up-to-date review of this evidence, with supporting sources, see R. First, J. Steele, and C. Gurney, *The*

South African Connection (London: Temple Smith, 1972 and Penguin paperback, 1973).

Two. The Heritage of Politics

1. A history told by J. D. Hargreaves, *The Prelude to the Partition of West Africa* (London: Macmillan, 1963).

2. The fact that Leopold knew almost nothing of the Congo Basin in no way dissuaded him from demanding, as he put it privately, this "slice of the magnificent African cake." When calling for recognition of his personal ownership of the greater part of that basin in 1884, his "effective occupation" was limited to a handful of tiny trading stations strung out along the Congo River as far as Stanley Falls. See J. Stengers, "King Leopold's Imperialism," in R. Owen and R. Sutcliffe, *Studies in the Theory of Imperialism* (London, 1972).

3. For this interesting though little-remembered figure, see J. Suret-Canale, "Un pionnier méconnu du mouvement démocratique et national en Afrique," *Etudes Dahoméennes,* Cotonou, 3 (December 1964).

4. Now Kinshasa, capital of Zaire.

5. Félix Eboué, quoted in B. Weinstein, *Eboué* (Oxford: Oxford University Press, 1972), p. 162.

6. Ibid.

7. When colonial governments duly passed to the founding of universities in Africa, they were above all careful to make sure that these should mirror the beliefs and teaching of their "mother universities" at Oxford and elsewhere. The first had evolved a self-conscious governing élite; the second must do the same. See the remarks of a distinguished British educationist, Sir Eric Ashby, in the 1964 Godkin Lectures at Harvard: "The founders of these universities worked in the belief that the social function of a university in Africa was to create and sustain an intellectual élite." And so it came about, and

with a vengeance. That in Ghana, he noted, had become "isolated from the life of the common people in a way which has had no parallel in England since the Middle Ages."

8. In 1952, for example, I traveled in Northern Nigeria as correspondent of the weekly *New Statesman*, whose politics were patently those of the British Labor party. But British officials in Kano and elsewhere seemed to think that nothing less fearsome or ferocious than the red hand of Bolshevism was knocking at their gates, or at least getting fingers into the lock, for they took care to impose on me a "conducting officer" who was supposed to go wherever I did. He was a nice old veteran called Captain Money, who soon concluded that the arrangement was embarrassing as well as silly, and so we arranged matters comfortably between ourselves. This kind of thing was also part of the late-colonial "atmosphere."

9. This, too, happened to me, again in 1952, in the French Soudan (Mali) after a visit to that most distinguished of French-speaking nationalists, the late Mamadou Konaté.

10. R. Wraith and E. Simpkins, *Corruption in Developing Countries* (London: Allen & Unwin, 1963).

11. *In Politique étrangère,* Centre d'Etudes de Politique étrangère, Paris, no. 4 (October 1954), p. 423.

12. The Senegalese Gabriel d'Arboussier in B. Davidson, "Jacobins in Africa," *History Today,* vol. 9, no. 2, London (February, 1959), p. 92.

13. Reviewed in detail by Yves Bénot, *Idéologies des Indépendances Africaines,* (Paris: Maspero, 1969), p. 120 ff.

14. In Niger (1970 population: about four million), the nationalist party led by Djibo Bakary came near to achieving it, but was frustrated by traditional chiefly opposition. See an article by Finn Fuglestad (interesting, though oddly written as if the star actor had passed from the scene, whereas he is living hale and hearty in Conakry, Guinea. There, in November 1970, Bakary and his wife escaped death at the hands of a Portuguese raiding force; these commandos battered down

the door of the Bakarys' house but failed to find the Bakarys):
"Djibo Bakary, the French and the Referendum of 1958," in
Journal of African History, 14, no. 2 (1973).

15. T. L. Hodgkin, "Towards Self-Government in West
Africa," in *The New West Africa*, ed. B. Davidson and A.
Ademola (London: Allen & Unwin, 1953), p. 96.

16. Also T. L. Hodgkin, circa 1951, but neither of us has
been able to find the context.

17. Not really a contentious point. For indications on precolonial institutions here, see, for example, M. G. Smith,
Government in Zazzau (Oxford: Oxford University Press,
1960).

18. O. Awolowo, *Path to Nigerian Freedom* (London:
Faber, 1947), p. 63.

19. Quoted in Kalu Ezera, *Constitutional Developments in
Nigeria* (Cambridge: at the University Press, 1960), p. 170.

20. Ezera, p. 199: "It must be stated . . . that it was
Nigerian leaders with only the reluctant consent of the
British Government, that created 'three states and two territories' for Nigeria at the London and Lagos Constitutional
Conferences (of 1954)." So true was this seen to be at the
time that even the fiery *West African Pilot* commented on
November 19, 1954, that: "The revised constitution is the
handiwork of Nigerians. Whatever may be the fault of the
British, they cannot be accused of having influenced the de-
cisions" of those constitutional conferences. So far had the
"inherited framework" now taken over.

21. Ezera, p. 250.

22. Quoted from G. Williams, "Social Stratification of a
Neo-Colonial Economy," in *African Perspectives*, ed. C. Allen
and R. W. Johnson (Cambridge: at the University Press,
1970), quoting from a forthcoming biography of Adelabu
by K. W. J. Post and G. Jenkins.

23. The counts were of treasonable felony and conspiracy.
For an extended account of this "most sensational trial in
Nigeria's legal history," see, e.g., L. K. Jakande, *The Trial of*

Obafemi Awolowo (London: Secker & Warburg; Lagos: John West, 1966).

24. C. Wrigley, quoted by Williams, "Social Stratification," p. 247.

25. Little evidence has survived. But a letter of May 30/ 31, 1967, written to another Nigerian (Dr. Tunji Otegbeye) by Major Chukwuma Nzeogwu, who had been prominent in this first coup of 1966, declares, for example, that "the control of all information media by the local capitalists and national bourgeoisie who manipulate our feuding war-lords, has sublimated the political sins of national disintegration and a return to the tribe." Quoted in *The Nigerian Vanguard,* April 1969, Birmingham, England.

What appears certain is that Nzeogwu and his fellow conspirators had no faith in secession and wished to retain Nigerian unity: see, for example, J. de St. Jorre, *The Nigerian Civil War* (London: Hodder, 1972), pp. 115, 167.

Three. The Force of Economics

1. W. W. Rostow, *The Stages of Economic Growth* (Cambridge: at the University Press, 1960), p. 4.

2. Ibid., p. 26.

3. P. A. Baran and E. J. Hobsbawm, reviewing Rostow's book in *Kyklos,* 14, no. 2 (1961).

4. Samir Amin, *L'Afrique de l'Ouest bloquée,* p. 70.

5. "I cannot emphasize too strongly at the outset" he wrote, "that the stages-of-growth are an arbitrary and limited way of looking at the sequence of modern history: and they are, in no absolute sense, a correct way." *(Stages of Economic Growth,* p. 1.) But it seems that he did not emphasize this strongly enough, and not only for the *Financial Times.*

6. B. Davidson, *In the Eye of the Storm: Angola's People,* pp. 357–358 and p. 301; and *in extenso* for a detailed discussion of the Angolan context.

7. United Nations General Assembly, A/8398/ Add. 1, December 5, 1971, p. 53.

8. And at the familiar cost, it appears, of a steady pauperization of the rural mass of Africans. A Portuguese investigation of 1971 went even further than Sutcliffe's findings for Southern Rhodesia (see footnote 14, Chapter One, above). In the relatively fertile west-central district of Huambo, during 1966-1970, gross earnings on African-owned farms were found to have fallen by an average of 35 percent in comparison with the previous five years, with consequences described as catastrophic. J. dos Cantos Carrico and J. A. de Morais, *Perspectivas do desinvolvimento regional do Huambo* (Nova Lisboa, Ist. de Investigação Agronomica de Angola, 1971), p. 23. I am grateful to Gerald Bender of the University of California at Los Angeles for drawing my attention to this report.

9. Constitutional eyewash in all questions of substance. Thus the "key revision" claims, remarkably enough on any rational scheme, that "the territories of the Portuguese Nation situated outside Europe constitute overseas provinces, which shall have their own statutes as autonomous regions"; and these regions may be called "autonomous states." All effective power remains, as before, in Lisbon. Detailed reports in, e.g., *Diário de Notícias,* Lisbon, July 1–9, 1971.

10. UN General Assembly, A/8398/ Add. 1, p. 40.

11. R. W. Clower, G. Dalton, M. Harwitz, A. A. Walters: *Growth Without Development* (Evanston: Northwestern University Press, 1966), e.g., pp. 5, 25 etc. See also B. Davidson, *In the Eye of the Storm: Angola's People,* Part Four.

12. This well-known phrase is that of John Barbot, writing in the late seventeenth century.

13. Cmd. 7638, 1895: "Correspondence relating to the Disturbances in Benin and the Operations against Chief Nana, 1894, (acting consul general Lagos, to foreign office).

14. Samir Amin, *L'Afrique de l'Ouest bloquée,* pp. 90, 206.

15. Ibid., pp. 206–207.

16. *West Africa,* March 12, 1973, p. 356.

17. P. C. Garlick, *African Traders and Economic Development in Ghana* (Oxford: Oxford University Press, 1971), quoted in *West Africa,* December 17, 1971.

18. Ibid.

19. Too strong? No serious observers seem to think so. Thus the international currency realignments of late 1972, for example, were described in the anything-but-radical *Mining Journal* as "a major fraud" perpetuated on the raw-material producers of the "developing" countries:

"Seen in its simplest terms, the industrialised nations have revalued and the developing nations, dependent on raw materials, have devalued. . . . The result is that raw materials will be cheaper for Europe and Japan; for the developing nations, their mineral wealth, in future, will buy fewer tractors, fewer hospitals, less food." Quoted in *West Africa,* January 14, 1972, p. 43. And if the "primary produce" price-inflation of 1973 may at first sight seem to deny this, a second look will show that inflation works both ways — for imports as well as for exports.

20. K. O. Dike, *Trade and Politics in the Niger Delta, 1830–1885* (Oxford: The Clarendon Press, 1956), p. 198.

21. O. Ikime, "Colonial Conquest and Resistance in Southern Nigeria," *Journal of the Historical Society of Nigeria,* 6, no. 3 (December 1972): 266.

22. Cf. the discussion by Ann Seidman, "Old Motives, New Methods . . . ," in *African Perspectives,* ed. Allen and Johnson, p. 256: "The Ghana government's heavy expenditure for the dam-smelter project, which contributed to the difficult economic circumstances in which it found itself in 1965, in reality has served primarily to provide an essential factor, cheap electric power, for the creation of another kind of export enclave." This project supplies power to a United States smelting consortium, and is obligated so to do for many years ahead, at a price which in 1969 was about *one-third* of the price paid by local Ghanaian consumers.

23. The "development myth" of the last decade or so, concludes the Brazilian economist Celso Furtado, "comes out as being only a new way of perpetuating colonialism." New industries "have become established in our countries on a pattern analogous to that of the old plantation economies . . ."; quoted by Romano Ledda, "Un nuovo risorgimento per l'America Latina?," *Rinascità,* Rome, April 13, 1973.

24. "African Affairs," *Journal of the Royal African Society,* 71 (January 1972).

25. S. R. Eyre, "Man the Pest: the Dim Chance of Survival," *New York Review of Books,* 17, no. 8 (November 18, 1971).

Four. Struggles to Escape

1. Sir A. Bryant, "The Nigerian Tragedy," *Illustrated London News,* January 24, 1970.

2. Cf. Bénot, *Idéologies des Indépendances Africaines,* for an extended discussion.

3. This began to change, at least among Marxist thinkers, early in the 1960s, when a real attempt to grapple with the realities of African socioeconomic structures saw its early initiatives. See, e.g., J. Suret-Canale, "Les Sociétés traditionelles en Afrique tropicale et le concept de mode de production asiatique," *La Pensée,* Paris, 117 (October 1964); and, extending the argument, C. Coquéry-Vidrovitch, "Récherches sur un mode de production africaine," *La Pensée,* 144 (April 1969), as well as Samir Amin and others in books cited earlier here. At the African end, meanwhile, and notably by the late Amilcar Cabral, there was much new and original analysis. See a preliminary collection of Cabral's writings, *Revolution in Guinea* (London: Stage One, and New York: Monthly Review Press, 1969), especially essays 5, 6 and 8.

4. London: Heinemann, 1967.

5. See J. L. Hymans, *Léopold Sedar Senghor* (Edinburgh:

Edinburgh University Press, 1971), especially pp. 179–199.

6. Speech of July 12, 1965, in *Bulletin* of Association pour l'Etude des Problèmes d'Outre-mer, no. 212; quoted by Bénot, p. 166.

7. See, e.g., R. H. Green and A. Seidman, *Unity or Poverty? The Economics of Pan-Africanism* (London and Baltimore: Penguin, 1968), and bibliography.

8. Quoted by Kalu Ezera, *Constitutional Developments in Nigeria,* pp. 24–27. On the personality and ideas of the National Congress of B.W.A., and its brief but interesting life, see an important book by J. Ayodele Langley, *Pan-Africanism and Nationalism in Western Africa, 1900–1945* (Oxford University Press, 1973).

9. As late as 1972, large states of the francophone sphere such as Malagasy were still trying to extricate themselves from direct French military influence or control.

10. Duri Mohammed, "Notes on the Common Market and Africa," in *Africa and the World,* ed. R. K. A. Gardiner, M. J. Anstee, and C. L. Patterson (Addis Ababa: Oxford University Press, 1970), pp. 122–127 (written in 1966).

11. Extensive discussion and documentation are in V. Bakpetu Thompson, *Africa and Unity* (London: Longman, 1969).

12. Very clearly, even by 1971, a record far less feeble in its effect than the opponents of such sanctions have liked to claim.

13. Quoted from press sources by B. Davidson, "Le Project de dialogue . . ." in *Le Monde Diplomatique,* Paris (June 1971).

14. Green and Seidman, pp. 141–144. For the background up to 1964, see also J. S. Nye, *Pan-Africanism and East African Integration* (Cambridge: Harvard University Press, 1965); and in a wider perspective, E. A. Brett, *Colonialism and Underdevelopment in East Africa: The Politics of Economic Change, 1919–1939* (New York: NOK Publishers Ltd., 1973).

15. Before being driven off, the raiders from Bissau attacked and partially wrecked Touré's residence, but the Presi-

dent was happily absent. On this occasion they also missed Amilcar Cabral, whose three-room bungalow in Conakry, where his wife and children lived, they likewise attacked.

16. Quoted from, and discussed in, Samir Amin, *Le développement inégal,* (Paris: Minuit, 1973), pp. 161–164. The whole book is an often brilliant discussion of "centre-periphery" relations and their consequences.

17. By 1970, such was the largely illegal emigration of Portuguese from Portugal during the 1960s, whether in flight from military service or in escape from poverty, that the region of Paris was now the third greatest urban concentration of Portuguese, after Libson and Oporto.

18. Widely documented. Cf., e.g., J. Marcum, "The United States and Portuguese Africa," *Africa Today,* 18, no. 4 (October 1971), who concludes that "the aggregate American involvement in Portugal's wars is more extensive and complex than is generally realized . . . [and has] resulted in a situation in which private interests have been permitted to redefine national policy from that of a rather limited to a massive intervention in support of the status quo." *Mutatis mutandis,* the same can be said of Britain, France, Federal Gemany, and, to a lesser extent Italy and Japan.

19. Samir Amin, *Le développement inégal,* where he develops the thesis that a given system "is not surpassed from its centre but from its periphery," and offers two examples: "the birth of capitalism at the periphery of the systems of the great pre-capitalist civilisations," Egypt and China, "and the crisis of today," where it is once again in the countries of "the periphery, confined within the limits of an ever more unequal development, that a decisive transformation of society may begin."

20. The first statement is of 1963, the second of 1966, both quoted in Bénot's richly documented book *Idéologies des Indépendances Africaines,* pp. 166–167.

21. Amilcar Cabral, quoted in B. Davidson, *The Libera-*

tion of Guiné (London and Baltimore: Penguin, 1969), p. 139.

Five. The Development of People

1. J. K. Nyerere, Report to TANU national conference (Dar es Salaam: Government Printer, September 1971), p. 22.

2. Quoted in *West Africa,* August 13, 1971.

3. *Nyerere,* p. 13.

4. I take the liberty of quoting this from a letter by Dr. Nyerere to me in 1972.

5. "Why does [African] agriculture remain so backward? What is wrong with those responsible for agriculture that they have so little to show to their credit? . . . First, there is a condition which most African countries have failed to fulfil or create, that of at least a minimum political link between the peasantry and the government. . . . So long as there is this lack of identification, it will be difficult to effect the radical changes necessary to transform agriculture. . . ." J. Dalton, "Shifting Perspectives of African Agriculture," in *Africa and the World,* ed. Gardiner, Anstee, and Patterson, pp. 96, 108.

6. See, e.g., a tentative appraisal from the radical side by I. G. Shivji, *Tanzania: The Silent Class Struggle,* with commentaries by W. Rodney, J. Saul, and T. Szentes. The issue of *Cheche,* the Tanzania student journal in which this was originally published in October 1970, was banned on the curious grounds, apparently, that the editors were trying to import "Russian socialism," instead of spreading "true Tanzanian socialism" (shades of "socialism in one country" à la Ahidjo in Cameroun), an act of suppressive censorship which explained much about the state of mind of those who imposed it. The appraisal was afterwards published, but again in English, by Zenit, Box 1156, Lund, Sweden.

7. Plowing by donkey was also considered, and again the difficulties were not small. On this point Mr. B. M. Gerard of the Edinburgh School of Agriculture has instructively noted that "Donkeys need little high quality food, but are difficult to handle. Bullocks are more suitable but still need experienced handlers to control them, and they also need good food throughout the year. About 100 bullocks will be needed for 400 acres of land to be ploughed, and will require 100 acres of pasture throughout the year, which means irrigating in the dry season in most parts of Tanzania, or supplementary feed brought in from other areas or from another country. . . ." Letter to author, March 9, 1972.

8. Our century's classic statement on this subject was made by Trotsky as early as 1904, and with a fearful prescience. See I. Deutscher, *The Prophet Armed* (Oxford: Oxford University Press, 1954), p. 90.

9. See D. Martin, "La Tanzanie par les livres," *Revue Française de Science Politique,* 23 (February 1973), 119. A corresponding interest could usefully be shown in the related efforts of some other African countries. One of these would be Somalia where, since 1969, another regime vowed to "anti-élitism" and "self-reliance" has grappled with the problems of the "neocolonial" inheritance, and, by all the signs, with interesting results.

10. Shivji, p. 26; he goes on, however, to point to contrary pressures and factors in the evolving Tanzanian situation.

11. The "ideological indicators" may be found in current documentation, and most succinctly in Nyerere's own reflections: e.g., *Education for Self-Reliance,* March 1967; *Socialism and Rural Development,* September 1967; *After the Arusha Declaration,* October 1967; and other statements, all Government Printer, Dar es Salaam.

12. The constitutional description of these countries was changed from "colonies" to "overseas provinces of Portugal" at the outset of the 1950s, when the government of Dr. Oliveira Salazar (since replaced by that of Professor Marcello

Caetano) desired to enter the United Nations without opening its colonial territories to UN inspection. See also footnote 9, Chapter Three.

13. Essential in a now considerable bibliography of the history and development of these movements are: A. Cabral, *Revolution in Guinea,* and other papers and lectures now in the course of preparation for publication in a collected edition; E. Mondlane, *The Struggle for Mozambique* (London and Baltimore: Penguin, 1969); numerous papers and statements by Agostinho Neto, M. de Andrade, and other leaders, notably M. dos Santos and Machel Samora of Mozambique, published in various journals since the late 1950s and especially in *Mozambique Revolution,* regular organ of the Mozambique Front of Liberation (FRELIMO), P.O. Box 15274, Dar es Salaam. See also B. Davidson, *The Liberation of Guiné* and *In the Eye of the Storm: Angola's People,* and books listed in these. On the particular point of absence of a "reformist option," see Davidson, "In the Portuguese Context," in *African Perspectives,* ed. Allen and Johnson.

On September 24, 1973, the independence of the State of Guinea-Bissau was proclaimed by a National Assembly elected on the basis of universal suffrage in areas throughout the country liberated from Portuguese control by the PAIGC. By December, 1973, this state was recognized by 75 member-states of the UN, as well as by the UN itself. For discussion of the internal background of this development, see B. Davidson, "African Peasants and Revolution," in *Jnl. of Peasant Studies,* i, 2, 1974 (London: Frank Cass). Basic constitutional texts are published by PAIGC, B.P. 298, Conakry, Guinea, and partially reproduced in "Growing from Grass Roots," CFMAG, 12 Little Newport St., London WC 2.

14. Valuable material on this point is in J. Marcum, *The Angolan Revolution* (Cambridge: M.I.T. Press, 1969), p. 49. See also chapters by A. Margarido and D. L. Wheeler in R. H. Chilcote, *Protest and Resistance in Angola and Brazil* (Berkeley: University of California Press, 1972).

15. A point well taken by Lisbon which, being faced with

military defeat, began in 1970 or thereabouts to contemplate precisely this kind of reform.

16. Mostly in Latin America. Aside from Che Guevara's *Bolivian Diary* (London: Lorimer; New York, 1968), perhaps the most instructive account of such an example is Hector Bejar's equally honest *Les guérillas péruviennes de 1965* (Paris: Maspero, 1969). See p. 79: "We go on marching by night, short of food, eating almost nothing. There's nothing left for us but to talk with the peasants," whose language is not Spanish, but Quechua. "We try, and are variously received: mistrust, fear. They all help us, but straight away one word separates us from them, 'papay.' The papay is the boss, white or mulatto, the foreigner. We must stop being 'papays': our salvation depends on it. But there's another barrier: the language. Few of us can talk Quechua . . . only one of us can talk it with the local pronunciation. . . ."

17. "But without it, nothing of lasting value can be done"; quoted in Davidson, *The Liberation of Guiné*, p. 52.

18. A. Cabral, "National Liberation and Culture," lecture at Syracuse University, New York, February 20, 1970. Forthcoming in collected edition of Cabral's works.

19. Ibid.

20. Ibid.

Index

Busia, Dr. Kofi, failure of government, 14, 105–106, 129

Cabinda Gulf Oil Corporation, 82
Cabral, Amilcar, 169, 171–176, 179, 191, 193
Cameroun, 53, 117
Cape Verde Islands, 126, 163–164, 182
capital assets, 77; developmental use, 24; of Angola, 83
capitalism: as African solution, 17, 49–52, 58–59, 65, 71, 74–77, 81–84, 90–91, 104, 146; in South Africa 31, 33; conditions for, 92–93; African rejection, 93–95, 99, 178–179; extension of world system, 99–100; colonial influence, 182; historical development, 193
caste economy, 32, 81
Chad, 72
China, failure of capitalism, 71
Chokwe, 11
Christaller, the Rev. J. G., 18
Christianity: policy for Africa, 48–49; African, 119
class stratification, 90, 115, 179
class struggle, 115
Clifford, Sir Hugh, 120–121, 125
Clifford Constitution of 1922 (Nigeria), 60
cocoa: 89, effect on Ghanaian economy, 5, 21–22, 105–106
coffee export, 21, 89, 149
Cold War, effect of, 47, 114
colonialism: basis of current structure, 3–5, 11, 15, 17, 21, 34–41, 45–50, 53–63, 70–71, 76–78, 80–83, 105, 109, 119 145, 164, 175; transition from, 6, 11, 17–18, 41–71; European-African interaction, 17, 37, 39–41, 86–88, 145; struggle against, 39–40, 112; value of, 111–112; necessity of break, 153; capitalism and, 182 See also development; nationalism
Common Market. See European Common Market; South African Common Market

Common Organization for Africa and Madagascar (OCAM), 133–134
Communauté Economique de l'Afrique de l'Ouest (CEAO), 134–135
communications, 157
communism (the Left), 47, 114–115, 118
community: need for, 8, 10–12; value of, 111. See also cooperation
Congo Basin, 34. See also Belgian Congo
Conseil de l'Entente, 134, 136
consumer goods, 154
consumption: food, 21; aim toward, 73
cooperation: among rural populations, 7–12, 158–161; regional, 130–137; exploitation, 154. See also unity, intra-African; unity, national
copper production, 23–24
corruption: in new regimes, 4, 29, 58, 66–67, 108–109; of capitalism, 51–52
cotton exports, 80, 149
cultural progress, 145, 159, 161, 167, 171–180
culture: ancient, 8; tribal, 56, 110, 171
currency crisis. See Ghana

Dahomey, 72, 134, 136
debt, to foreign countries, 5, 14, 27, 30–31, 78, 100, 106
decolonization, 17–18, 40–41, 44–66, 120. 126
democracy: as model, 49–52, 59, 70, 76, 140; failure, 110; new organizations of, 166, 171, 178–179
development: foreign attitudes about, 3–4, 45, 181; incapability, within existing structure, 4–5, 30–31, 78, 92, 105; growth and production without, 5, 16, 23–24, 28, 79–85, 87–92, 105, 138, 150–151, 153, 184; transition

149; nationalization, 155; inflation, 190

income. *See* wages

independence. *See* nationalism

"Indirect Rule," 39

industrial revolution, 25, 75, 87, 154

industry: division between Africa and West, 25–29; development, 31, 102–103, 155; in South Africa, 81; Third World production, 138

inflation, 190. *See also* Ghana: currency crisis

instability, 141

institutional crisis, 6, 13–14; historical background, 15–18; responsibility for, 106–109. *See also* structures, national

international system. *See* foreign interests

investment: private, 30; manufacturing 92–95; African, 95. *See also* foreign aid

Iron Age, 15, 19, 182

Islam, influence of, 16

Ivory Coast, 38, 71, 94, 129; effect of export crops, 21; economic growth, 89–91; regional cooperative efforts, 134–136

Ja Ja of Opobo, 88, 96–97

Japanese development, 77–78

Kano riots, 64, 67

Kaunda, Kenneth, 101, 132

Kenya, 41, 48 115; decolonization, 57–58; experimental self-rule, 116–117; regional cooperation, 130–132; relation of education to labor, 151

Kenyatta, Jomo, 41

labor: in money economy, 23–24; immigrant, 24, 80; quantity of, 28, 90; skilled black, 32–33; "contract" system, 79; cheap, 82; effect of slave trade on, 86; in relation to schooling, 151–152.

Lagos, Nigeria, 65

land use, 152–153

Latin America, 99–100, 143

leadership: irresponsibility, 4, 29, 67, 106, 108–109; federation as ideal, 53–54; anticapitalistic, 65; revolutionary, 117–118, 166–170, 173; offensive attitude, 159. *See also* élitist leadership; traditionalism

leftist influence. *See* communism

Leopold II, King, 38, 185

Lesotho, 34

liberation movements. *See* revolutionary movements

Liberian economy, 83–85, 88–89

life expectancy, 148

linguistic alienation, 121

Luchazi, 11

Lunda, 11

Luvale, 11

MacPherson constitution of 1951 (Nigeria), 62–63

Malagsy, 192

Malawi, 34

Mali, 46, 72, 116, 123; economic cooperation attempt, 132–134, 136

manufacture: lack of African investment, 92–95; exploitation, 154

markets, world: effect on Africa, 20–24, 101–102

Martin, David, 181

Marxism, 115, 191. *See also* communism

Mauritania, 132–133, 136

Mboya, Tom, 115

Mbunda, 11

media, 188

Mensah, J. H., 149

micronationalism. *See* tribal nationalism

"middle-class solution," 48–52, 56, 58–59, 64–66, 70–71, 74, 80–81, 85, 89–91, 109, 146, 178

military conscription, 169–170

military cooperation, 11

military power, 13, 59, 69–70, 110

minerals, 77, 80, 98–99

modification. *See* structures, national

socialism
political control, European, 97, 120–122
"poor" countries (Third World): influenced by "rich," 3–4, 30; inequality, 25–26, 137–138, 190; world interdependence, 139
population growth, 15, 17, 19–20; relation to food, 22–23, 153; Ivory Coast 90; under 25 years old, 179
Portuguese territories, 126, 189; revolt in, 11–12, 139–140, 163–176, 178, 183, 193
poverty, 77, 156
power concentration of, 109
price structure, world, 25–26, 30
primary producers, 25–27, 81, 98, 138, 190
private enterprise. See capitalism
production: without development, 5, 23–24, 27–28, 84, 153, 160; in relation to population, 20; level of, 21, 25, 148; for export, 21–25, 27, 152; theories of, 73; fails to meet demand, 151; handicapped by old methods, 159–160. See also food production; primary producers
progress. See development

racism. See apartheid system
radicalism. See revolution, as instrument of change; revolutionary movements
railway, Tanzania/Zambia, 132
Rassemblement Démocratique Africain (RDA), 53–54, 119
reformism, 61; inadequacy, 14, 19, 75, 109, 146, 150–151, 164–166; historical, 16; colonial influence, 37, 114; value, 111–112
regionalism. See tribal nationalism
religion: influence of, 11–12; taboos, rejection of, 171
resources, 19, 71; African ownership, 24, 156; exhaustion of, 102–103
revolution, as instrument of change, 75, 118, 143, 153, 157, 161–180
revolutionary movements: in Portuguese colonies, 10–12, 126–127, 140, 163–174, 176, 178; lack of support, 128–129
Rhodesia, 51, 126, 176. See also Zambia
"rich" countries: influence on "poor," 3–4, 30, 190; international division with "poor," 25–26
Richards Constitution of 1946 (Nigeria), 62
Rostow, Walt W., 72–75, 77–78, 83, 99, 147
rural populations: cooperative efforts, 154–155, 158–160, 163, liberation, 170; economic decline, 184
Rwanda, 131

self-confidence, of Africans, 110–113, 172
self-reliance, 155
self-rule: frictions, 5; weaknesses, 29; reasons for failure, 105–110; value of, 110–114, 135, 145–147. See also nationalism
Senegal, 114, 117, 123; economic stagnation, 28–29, 92; economic cooperation effort, 132–134, 136
Senegal River 132–133, 137
Senghor, Léopold, 53, 114, 117, 133, 136, 141–142
settlers. See white-settlers
Sharpeville massacre, 31
Sierra Leone, 120
slave trade: effect of, 16, 86–88, 182
slums, 17
social services, 24, 151
social values, 152
socialism, 114, 116–117, 137, 158
society: absence of change, 89; class stratification, 90; based on community, 110; effect of education on, 151–152; revolutionary restructuring, 161–163, 165–180
socioeconomic system, 144; based on past, 4–5, 70; expansion, 154; stagnation, 182. See also economics, African; nationalism; society

Somalia, 41, 126
South Africa, Republic of: foreign aid effect, 31–35; industrialization, 81; measures against, 126; African attitude towards, 129; liberation movement, 176, 183
South African Common Market, 33
"spread effects," 184
Stages of Economic Growth (Rostow), 72
stagflation, 32
standards of living, 153
structures, national: based on colonial system, 3–5, 11, 15, 17, 21, 34–41, 45–59, 65, 76–77, 81–83, 97–98, 128, 145, 156, 159, 164; subject to international system, 4, 31–35, 78–79, 89–92, 94–95, 100–105, 109, 137–138, 146–147; necessity for change, 5, 20, 131, 154, 161; crisis, 13, 15, 17; historical dimension, 15–16, 37, 74–75; values, 111–112; future subordination, 137–138; modification, 146–147, 149. *See also* development; nationalism
Sudan, the, 16, 182; decolonization, 46
Sutcliffe, R. B., 184
Swaziland, 34
systems. *See* institutional crisis; structures, national

"take-off," 73, 75, 99, 102, 104, 147
Tanganyika, 48. *See also* Tanzania
TANU, 8, 169, 175–176, 178
Tanzania: cooperative villages, 7–10; British measures against, 101; regional unification, 130–132; progress report, 147–149; education, 152, 155; land use, 152–153; socioeconomic movement, 155-163, 168, 174–176
Tanzania African National Union (TANU), 8, 169, 175–176, 178
technology: identified with progress, 3; level of, 15, 23; exploitation, 154
Third World problems, 4. *See also* "poor" countries

Togo, 53–55, 72, 99, 103; regional cooperation, 134, 136
Touré Sékou, 101, 133–134, 192
trade, unfavorable terms, 24, 28, 78. *See also* exports; imports; slave trade
traditionalism: departure from, 7, 10–12, 16, 17, 153, 166, 177; as political factor, 36; interaction with colonial powers 37, 39, 45–46, 52–63
transition period. *See* nationalism
Transkei, 34
tribal attitudes, elimination of, 171
tribal nationalism (micronationalism; regionalism), 5, 53, 55–57, 61–70, 110, 142, 154, 188. *See also* cooperation
Tubman, Pres. William V. S., 84
Turay, Samori, 16

Uganda, 48, 130
underdevelopment. *See* development
unemployment, 26
United Nations, 53, 127, 132, 196
United States: reproaches Africans, 52; domination, in Liberia, 83–85; involvement in Portugal's wars, 193
United States Agency for International Development, 84
unity, intra-African: historical background, 40–42, 119; Pan-Africanism, 41, 119, 124; as solution to problems, 118–119; scorned, 120–121; practice versus theory, 122–123, 154; experiments in, 123–124; progress toward, 124–129, 173, 179; basis, 141–142; among liberation movements, 176
unity, national, 53–55, 57–58, 141–142, 154, 173. *See also* cooperation; Nigeria: evolution of independence; unity, intra-African
Upper Volta, 134, 136
uranium, 98–99
urban expansion, 17, 31, 33, 90–91, 103, 142, 152, 154, 184

value systems. *See* social values

Verwoerd, Prime Minister Hendrik, 33
Vietnam, 168
villages, cooperative, 9–12, 152, 158–161, 176
Volta Republic, 90, 123. *See also* Upper Volta

wages: low rate, 23–25; improvement in, 32, 138; inequality, 184
waGogo, resettlement to cooperative villages, 7–10, 176–177
water shortage, 7–10
wealth: usable, 25, 137; transfer from poor to rich, 28, 30–31, 35, 88, 90, 100; potential, 77
West: attitudes about Africa, 4, 45, 101–102, 106–108, 118; developmental gap with Africa, 25–26. *See also* foreign aid; foreign interests

West Africa, 46, 182; regional cooperation, 132–137. *See also* British West Africa; French West Africa
white-settlers, economic situation of, 81–82
wine imports, 81
women, social inferiority, 172
work, old methods, 160
World War II, 47

Zaire, 126
Zambia (Northern Rhodesia), 34; production without development, 23–24, 80, 83; economic cooperation, 131–132
Zanzibar, 38, 48, 130
Zanzibari Coast, 16
Zimbabwe, 176
Zulu empire, 16
Zululand, 34